OPERATION
OTTER

OPERATION OTTER

PHILIP WAYRE

Chatto & Windus
LONDON

By the same author

A Guide to the Pheasants of the World
Wind in the Reeds
The River People
Lutra, the Story of an Otter
The Private Life of the Otter
All About Otters

Published in 1989 by
Chatto & Windus Ltd
30 Bedford Square
London WC1B 3SG

A CIP catalogue record for this book is available from the British Library.

ISBN 0-7011-3402-X

Photoset by Rowland Phototypesetting Ltd
Bury St Edmunds, Suffolk
Printed in Great Britain by
Redwood Burn Ltd
Trowbridge, Wiltshire

For Jeanne, without whose constant help and encouragement there would be no Otter Trust and no *Operation Otter*.

Acknowledgements

This book is a joint effort in that my wife, Jeanne, has not only provided help and advice, but much useful criticism as well. Over the years she has assumed responsibility for the management of the Otter Trust: its continued success and hence this book have been the tangible result of her skill, hard work and enthusiasm.

I also wish to record my grateful thanks to every member of staff at the Otter Trust, both at Earsham and at North Petherwin in Cornwall as well as at the Norfolk Wildlife Park, all of whom have contributed to the Otter Trust's achievements.

The successful re-introduction of young otters into the wild would not have been possible without the constant advice, encouragement and practical help of the Nature Conservancy Council and I am especially grateful to Dr Don Jefferies, Chief Scientist Directorate, and his colleagues who have been directly involved with the re-introduction project since its beginning in 1983.

I am also grateful to the other organisations who have provided assistance: the County Naturalists' Trusts, especially the Norfolk Naturalist Trust, the Vincent Wildlife Trust and the Royal Society for Nature Conservation.

Finally I wish to record my thanks to all those field workers and scientists who have given me the benefit of their advice, personal observations and opinions.

Together with my publishers I am grateful to the following for their permission to reproduce material. To David & Charles for the world map on p. 16, from *Otters in Britain* by Liz Laidler; to Croom Helm for the chart on p. 51, from *The Natural History of Otters* by Paul Chanin; and to the Vincent Wildlife Trust for the map on p. 19.

Contents

Introduction

According to my mother, the air in the Thames Valley was enervating. In the early 1930s it was also heavy with depression, a trade recession which brought gloom to our household as grey as the night mist rising from the river.

Perhaps it was this atmosphere rather than any misanthropic tendency which led me as a small boy to escape as often as possible into the relative solitude of our suburban garden. The summer nights, I recall, were laden with the scent of lavender and sweet-smelling phlox. Armed with a simple hurricane lamp and a butterfly net, I hunted for moths lured from the herbaceous border by the light from my lamp.

In the gloaming the rockery was transformed in my mind to an escarpment in the Himalayas, our neighbour's cat into a lurking leopard waiting to pounce on me, while the slow worm caught for an instant in the swaying shadows wore a cobra's hood. The tawny owl's hoot sent a shiver of fear down my spine.

My nightly wanderings were a source of mystery to my brother and sister, both some years older, and were tolerated without curiosity by my parents.

This need for solitude and interest in animals continued at my preparatory school in Ewell where, with the help of Jones Minor, I caught rats beneath the ground-floor rooms accessible to a very small boy by squeezing under the floor joists adjacent to the cellar. I kept the rats as pets in a homemade cage.

It was at my public school in Dorset that my fascination for wild creatures grew into a serious hobby, and the greater freedom accorded to pupils allowed me more opportunity to wander into the nearby country-side with a tame kestrel or a ferret for company. As soon as I was old

British otter in a pool on a North Norfolk marsh.

enough to drive a car, I was able to fulfil my long-held ambition to pursue the wild ducks and geese on the saltings and mudflats of the Wash.

Shooting wigeon under the moon was my favourite pastime, and I liked nothing better than to be alone in the darkness far out at the salting's edge, crouched amongst the sea lavender, my waders squelching in the black mud, while I waited for the moon to rise and the oncoming tide, already hissing gently in the creek, to rise enough to move the ducks from distant sandbars and send them flying in to feed on the short sweet grass behind me.

One June morning, long before the first sign of dawn, I was out at the tide edge near the mouth of the Stiffkey river in north Norfolk hoping to make some sound recordings before the noise of aircraft and distant traffic made this impossible. I had followed the river as it coiled through the lush grazing meadows, where bullocks stood knee-deep in the night mist, making the air heavy with their sweet-sour breath, to the grass-grown sea wall, and the great sluice-gate where the river made its final bow to the land before losing its identity in the tidal maze of creeks and gulleys carved in the gleaming mud of the saltings, a land of sea lavender, sea aster and gold-dusted purslane.

Dawn came quickly and with it a chill breeze, dispersing the mist. Soon the sandwich terns left the point to follow the tide with harsh cries in search of sand eels and fry. Busy oystercatchers trilled their spring song, carmine bills half-open and pointing down at the golden sand as the male birds circled their mates.

As I watched the muddy water of the estuary merge with the first wavelets along the shore, I became aware of a creature moving in from the sea, only to disappear almost immediately. I crouched low in my creek, well hidden by the sea lavender, when the otter surfaced again just below me and continued its way upstream. Again it dived with effortless ease, and this time came up within ten paces of me. I froze and hardly dared to breathe as its flattened head turned towards me and I heard its snort of surprise and watched the graceful arc of its body and rudder as it slipped down beneath the surface. I saw it no more, but the seed of curiosity had been sown.

British otter running on the North Norfolk mud flats.

CHAPTER 1

The Making of a Wildlife Park

Many naturalists of the old school, and I can no longer pretend to belong to anything else, had their interest in wildlife aroused by the desire to kill things, and I was no exception. Like many before me I began by collecting wildfowl which had been wing-tipped either by accident or design during my shooting expeditions. The joy those first birds brought me, and the interest aroused by studying their individual characteristics and getting to know them eventually led to my giving up the gun in favour of the camera. This change led to a period when I spent much of my time making wildlife films for television. But long before that, when coming out of the Navy in my early twenties, I had to decide what to do with my life. Although born in Surrey I had become addicted to East Anglia, and particularly to the desolate sandbars of the Wash and the wide saltings of the north Norfolk coast, where I had pursued the wintering flocks of wigeon and brent geese.

The war over, I decided to return to Norfolk. Farming was the only occupation which appeared to lead in that direction. Within a year I became pupil to a well-known farmer in Oxfordshire for a period before returning to Norfolk to work on a large arable farm near Fakenham. Two years later my parents set me up on a farm of my own at Mileham, and there I continued to build up my collection of waterfowl. The farm was an ill-fated venture, largely because I was a failure as a farmer, and five years later my wife and I had moved to a much smaller farm at Great Witchingham, where I concentrated on breeding turkeys at about the time that Bernard Matthews, who is now perhaps the world's largest turkey breeder, was also setting up his enterprise not two miles away. My heart was never really in poultry farming, and when in the early 1960s Anglia Television started in Norwich I jumped at the chance of presenting local natural history programmes. These required the appearance in the studio of tame animals, and so my collection began to grow. Some six years later my entire stock of breeding turkeys contracted fowl pest and had to be destroyed on the orders of the Ministry of Agriculture. I recall the revulsion I felt at the sight of a digger excavating a pit the size of a small swimming pool and twice as deep, into which thousands of carcases were hurled by men in protective clothing. However, once the shock and the despair had worn off, I realised there was one consolation, and that was the compensation paid by the government.

For some years people had shown an increasing interest in my animal collection, and slowly a plan began to form in my mind. Unimpressed by urban zoos, I wanted to establish a wildlife collection in natural surroundings where the mammals and birds would be kept in large open enclosures or aviaries, landscaped and planted with trees, where visitors

Young little owls bred in the Norfolk Wildlife Park.

The little owl introduced into Britain about 70 years ago has successfully established itself.

and especially children could see and study them. Even in those days it had already become apparent that much of the world's wildlife, including our own, was threatened with extinction and that positive efforts would have to be made if many species were to survive at all. I felt that a collection rather on the lines of Whipsnade Zoo, but even more natural, could play an important role, since people would become more interested in the plight of wildlife if they could see breeding groups of animals kept under almost natural conditions. I also felt strongly that in the case of some species it ought to be possible to breed numbers in captivity with the ultimate aim of reintroducing individuals into the wild, either to boost a failing wild population or to re-establish one, provided suitable habitat could be found and the animals' future safety ensured. Though belittled by some scientists, this seemed to me to be a very practical contribution to conservation and one which ought to become the aim of every zoo and wildlife collection.

Thus it was that in 1961 the Norfolk Wildlife Park came into being. I think I can claim to be the first person to coin the term 'wildlife park', and at the time I thought it described what I planned to do rather well. I described the setting up of the Park in the final chapters of my book *Wind in the Reeds*, named after a film of the same title I had made a few years before, but of course there have been many changes over the years. Almost the first and possibly the most important was our decision to keep only British and European mammals and birds, apart from domestic species kept largely to interest very young children and to give them the chance of more intimate contact with animals.

The collection still remains today much as it was twenty-six years ago, with few additions, although on the whole we tend to keep more individuals and fewer species, while concentrating on those which either have considerable public interest or educational potential or are endangered in the wild. My original belief that animals could be kept and bred in captivity for subsequent reintroduction into the wild has been borne out on a modest scale with species like the barn owl and the little owl, both of which have been bred regularly at Great Witchingham and released in East Anglia, and also with the European eagle owl, with which we have always had good breeding results, producing ninety-one young owls since the opening of the Park. Of these thirty-three young have been presented to the Swedish and German Conservation Authorities, both of whom have successfully reintroduced this magnificent bird into their forests, where it used to occur, but had become extinct. Releasing a captive-bred animal is never easy, but the Swedes have perfected a technique for the reintroduction of eagle owls which has worked well over many years. The first release took place in 1956, when a pair of eagle owls from Skansen were placed in a large aviary built in the

European eagle owl in the Norfolk Wildlife Park.

forest where the reintroduction was to take place. When their young were able to fly they were released from a trap-door in the roof of the aviary. At first they remained in the area of their parental home, often perching on top of the aviary. Gradually their exploring flights took them further afield, and finally their visits back home became irregular. This pattern of behaviour was repeated by other young owls subsequently raised in the same aviary. The birds turned wild, occupied their own territories in the vicinity and spread into the Kilsbergen area nearby, and to other suitable habitats in the same region. This successful attempt to reintroduce eagle owls was followed by similar schemes in other parts of southern Sweden.

The serious decline in the number of barn owls, especially in eastern England, has been well documented, and this species has always been bred at Great Witchingham for release in East Anglia. Since its foundation the Park has bred fifty-three barn owls, and of these twenty-two young birds have been released. Two methods of reintroduction have been tried, and both appear to have been successful. The first is identical to the Swedish method of reintroducing eagle owls, where young birds are released from the aviary in which they were bred. Like the eagle owls the young barn owls rarely wander very far, but settle down in the immediate vicinity. The second method has been to place young owls, about five weeks old, in a nesting box in a suitable barn or high up in a tree. It is important to place the young owlets in the nest-box well before they are able to fly, and food is then provided daily, but otherwise they are disturbed as little as possible. Once they become fully-fledged and have left the nest-box, food is supplied on a daily basis for as long as they return for it.

Of the sixty little owls bred in the Park thirty-two have been released into the wild in East Anglia, using the same methods. It has become apparent that little owls released from the aviaries in which they have been bred tend to occupy territories closer to home.

The Park soon acquired a reputation for its successful breeding of British mammals, including wild cats, foxes, badgers and otters. In 1974 a friend, seeing that we had two young badger cubs, asked what we

Young eagle owls in the Norfolk Wildlife Park.

proposed to do with them, and suggested that they should be released on his estate in west Norfolk, where badgers used to occur but had been destroyed by a previous owner. I was delighted with the idea and could think of no better future for our young badgers than a life in the wild. A release pen was built about 10 yards square, consisting of a chain-link fence, 4 feet high and buried about 2 feet in the ground. The two cubs were put in the enclosure on 30 December 1974, shortly before their mother gave birth to three more cubs in the Park. The young badgers started digging as soon as they were in the pen, and in a couple of weeks they had constructed quite a substantial sett with two large piles of earth outside the two entrances and with room underground for almost two bales of straw which was provided for bedding. The badgers stayed in the pen until 6 February, when they dug their way out under the wire, but they returned to their sett before daybreak. By early summer it was clear that the badgers had moved on, and contact with them was subsequently lost.

We decided to try again with the next three cubs, and they were put in the same enclosure in January 1976. Fed on freshly-shot rabbits, carrots, apples and sometimes a few dead day-old chicks, they too quickly settled down. Like their predecessors these badgers also burrowed under the wire after a few weeks, but they stayed in their sett and after several months the pen was slowly and carefully dismantled. I think we were all surprised at how readily the captive-bred badgers had settled down to a perfectly natural wild existence. They began burrowing the moment they were released from their crates, and only a few days later they were behaving like badgers reared in the wild. Soon they took to digging out rabbits and a wasps' nest nearby, but left a pheasant to hatch off successfully from a nest just 20 feet from the main entrance to their sett. To crown it all one of them gave birth to three cubs early in 1978, all of which were successfully reared, thus establishing the start of a new colony. This was probably the first recorded breeding in the wild by badgers that were themselves born in captivity.

Because of its sedentary habits and strong attachment to its home sett, the badger is a comparatively easy animal to study and we had no difficulty in monitoring the breeding success of our introduced animals. This was not to be the case with another British mammal, the otter, which by the early 1960s was already taking the downward plunge towards extinction in most parts of lowland Britain.

The policy of displaying animals in large enclosures quickly achieved notable breeding successes, among them the first British brown hare to be bred in captivity in Britain and the first Alpine ibex, stone curlews and wheatears to be bred here. For these and other outstanding breeding results the Park was awarded many medals and certificates from organisations including the World Wildlife Fund, the Avicultural Society and the Federation of Zoological Gardens. Gratifying though these results were, they had to be kept in perspective, and their real value would be known only if and when it became possible to use the knowledge gained to further the conservation of that particular species in the wild. Often the Park was the only collection in Britain, if not the world, keeping and endeavouring to breed a good many European or British species, so competition in the breeding stakes was lacking – a kind of one-horse race.

Looking back over more than a quarter of a century of running a specialised wildlife park, one fact stands out above all others, and that is the complete change in attitude towards wildlife of the average visitor, coupled with a far wider range of knowledge and a degree of sophistication unknown in those early years; and of course the youngsters of today are more knowledgeable, enquiring, and often more demanding than their parents when it comes to keeping animals in captivity.

My own view too has been moulded by time, so that over the years the enclosures in the Park have tended to get bigger, more and more emphasis is placed on breeding groups of animals and above all on educating and informing our visitors. We have given up keeping animals to which we thought we were unable to do justice, or which did not appear to be thriving. Among the first to go were our European brown bears; huge and magnificent though they were, we felt they should have acres of enclosure in which to roam, not a space the size of a large tennis court. (Indeed, the only bear enclosure I have seen in any zoo which is large enough is the brown bears' enclosure at Whipsnade.) Next to go were the wolves, the very rare Pyrenean race of the European wolf, a sub-species in danger of extinction in the wild. I had hoped that we would be able to breed them regularly and could perhaps persuade the Spanish authorities to co-operate in a reintroduction programme. In reality, although they had nearly an acre of pine woodland in which to roam, and while they were able to dig their own dens, they never looked really happy and we bred only one cub.

In those early days our common seals, kept in one of the largest seal pools in any zoo in Europe, were a great attraction, but although the pool held over a quarter of a million gallons of water which was changed every week there was something about keeping such active and intelligent animals as seals in this way which caused me a certain unease. I know that my wife, Jeanne, felt the same, and indeed it was she who originally suggested that we should no longer keep the brown bears and wolves. So, despite the fact that the Park was the first place in Britain where the common seal had bred and successfully reared its young in captivity, they too were phased out, and we now have only one aged specimen, the last of its line.

It was in the Park's early days that I first became enthralled by otters. At that time I was making a film about the wildlife of the Norfolk Broads called *Wind in the Reeds*, and I needed a pair of otters to feature in it. Otters were not at that time protected in this country, and there was

North American otters.

Common seal suckling its pup in the Seal Pool.

nothing to stop anyone taking young otter cubs should they be fortunate enough to find them. I anticipated little trouble in securing a pair, and proceeded to advertise in a number of newspapers and journals offering a fairly high reward for cubs brought to me in good condition. I could hardly believe it when after running the advertisements for several months I had not received a single reply. Eventually, in desperation, I was forced to import a pair of North American otters, which, although an entirely different species, are not too dissimilar from the British otter, at least to the uninitiated. I kept the North American otters after I had finished filming them and they subsequently produced cubs in the Park.

By then I was hooked on otters, and more determined than ever to keep and breed the British otter. Help towards that goal came from an unexpected quarter. At that time, the early 1950s, the coypu-catching campaign was at its height. Originally coypu were imported into East Anglia from South America and were farmed for their fur, called 'nutria'. Although looking like rats, coypu are more closely related to beavers and have webbed hind feet, are very good swimmers and can stay under water for up to twenty minutes. The female coypu's teats are situated on each of her flanks just above the waterline when she is swimming. This enables the young coypu to suckle while the family floats, rather like submarines refuelling alongside a depot ship. Crepuscular and nocturnal in its activity, the coypu makes runs amongst marsh plants and builds piles of vegetation to serve as nests as well as digging burrows in riverbanks, although these are usually not extensive.

Escaped animals eventually became a pest, and were caught in large box traps set by an army of Ministry of Agriculture coypu trappers. Such was the vast number of traps set nightly in the waterways of East Anglia, particularly in the Broads area, that I suppose it was inevitable that some otters should be caught, not attracted by the bait, usually carrots, potatoes and other vegetables, but simply by wandering into the traps, possibly out of curiosity. As soon as I heard this was happening I offered a substantial reward to any trapper bringing me a live otter unharmed. Hitherto they had usually shot the otter and sold it for its skin, worth at that time about £5. In this way I obtained a number of young, healthy otters, some of which I kept to form a breeding nucleus while the rest I released again on nearby rivers. The first cubs were born to these otters in 1970 and were the first British otters to be bred in captivity in Britain for eighty-nine years.

Coypu.

• OTTER FACTS •

● The otter's coat is usually chestnut brown in colour and paler on the underside, with varying amounts of white on the chin and throat. The intensity of the brown can vary considerably from individual to individual, some otters being pale grey-brown while others are almost black. White, off-white or partially white individuals have been recorded from time to time and these albinos or semi-albino otters seem to have turned up more frequently in Ireland on the River Shannon and along the west coast of Scotland in the vicinity of Mull, Islay and Jura.

● The otter's footprint or 'seal' is easily identifiable. The five widely separated toes may not all show up clearly, but the rounded appearance of the print and the ball under the sole of the foot, together with the flattening of the ridges between the toes caused by the inter-digital webs can be clearly distinguished.

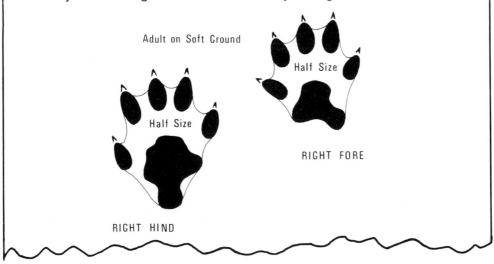

Adult on Soft Ground

Half Size

Half Size

RIGHT FORE

RIGHT HIND

• OTTER FACTS •

- Not all otter species have webs between their toes. The Asian short-clawed otter and the African clawless otter *Aonyx capensis* lack any skin there, giving their five rubbery 'fingers' the remarkable dexterity needed in feeling for their prey – small crustacea and molluscs hidden in rocky crevices or under stones on the riverbed.

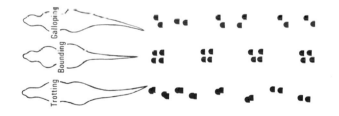

- On land otters appear rather awkward, though they can attain a surprising turn of speed – as much as 15mph. When walking the head and neck are held low with the hips and lower back arched, giving a humped appearance. The tail is extended straight behind and kept just above the ground. The apparent awkwardness of movement on land is caused by the back legs being twice as long as the front ones. When walking, an otter places the hind foot behind the track of the forefoot and when trotting, the hind foot usually falls on or close to the track left by the forefoot. The otter's normal gait on land is a kind of lope or canter, and there is great variation in its tracks, but if moving fast the track of the hind foot falls in front of that left by the forefoot. These tracks often appear more or less in pairs.

Jeanne with two otter cubs.

One day a young female otter was brought in, and because of the rather reddish tinge to her coat we named her Ginger. In due time she produced a litter of cubs which she reared successfully. However, four weeks after the birth of her third litter disaster struck. I happened to be passing her enclosure at dusk and saw that she was lying at the edge of the pool, lapping the water like a cat; but it was her hind legs that attracted my attention, for while the rest of her body looked quite normal her hindquarters had turned over and appeared to be lying limp and useless. I called her name, and her natural reaction was to return to her den and her two cubs, but it then became painfully clear that both hind legs were totally paralysed and she could only drag herself along by her front legs.

Our veterinary surgeon soon confirmed our worst fears. The paralysis was due to a spinal injury and nothing could be done to help her. With a sad heart I agreed that the only thing to do was to put her to sleep. The cubs were fully dependent on her milk and were still very small, with their eyes just beginning to open. Jeanne took them in and fed them from a kitten-rearing bottle. For the next few weeks our house and especially the kitchen where we kept the cubs was invaded by the familiar musky smell of young otters. Christened Lucy and Kate, both grew apace, developing into fine healthy young animals which were also delightfully tame. As well as having the run of the house for much of the day both of them enjoyed an evening walk around the Park with us, trundling along at our heels like small clockwork toys, occasionally bumping into each other and falling over only to pick themselves up and hurry on in their determination not to get left behind.

In the years to come Kate produced several litters of cubs and founded a dynasty, but with poor little Lucy fate was to prove less generous.

Kate and Lucy at twelve weeks.

CHAPTER 2

The Otter – An Introduction

Right:
Male Eurasian otter
stretched to his full height.

World distribution of otter
species.

Otters occur in almost every part of the world except Australia and New Zealand, Madagascar, and the Arctic and Antarctic regions. According to C. J. Harris in his book *Otters* (1968), there are nineteen accepted species and very many more sub-species or races. However, classification of many of these sub-species appears to have been based on too little scientific evidence and too few specimens to be valid. The common otter *Lutra lutra* inhabits the streams, rivers, lakes, marshes

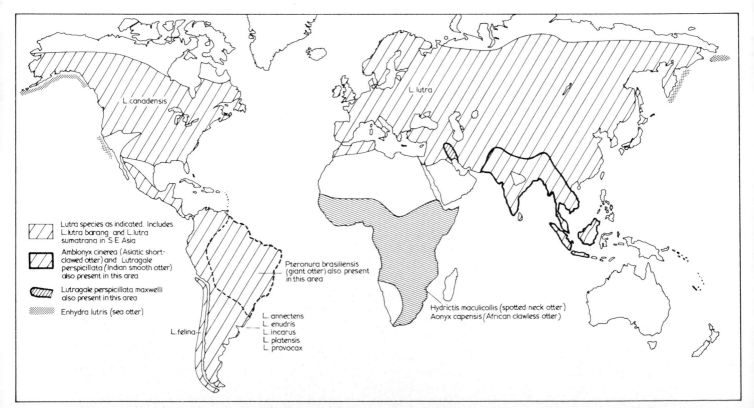

L. canadensis

L. lutra

Lutra species as indicated. Includes L. lutra barang and L. lutra sumatrana in S.E. Asia

Amblonyx cinerea (Asiatic short-clawed otter) and Lutragale perspicillata (Indian smooth otter) also present in this area

Lutragale perspicillata maxwelli also present in this area

Enhydra lutris (sea otter)

Pteronura brasiliensis (giant otter) also present in this area

Hydrictis maculicollis (spotted-neck otter)
Aonyx capensis (African clawless otter)

L. annectens
L. enudris
L. incarus
L. platensis
L. provocax

L. felina

and coasts of Britain and Ireland, and its range spreads right across Europe and Asia extending from Northern India, China, Japan and Taiwan as far north as the Arctic Circle. Southwards its range extends into South-East Asia, to the Malay Peninsula and through the eastern islands of Sri Lanka and Java. It is found all around the shores of the Mediterranean, throughout the Middle East and westwards to Morocco and Algeria. It is not surprising that with such a vast distribution the common otter has evolved into a number of sub-species or races, most of which occur in eastern and southern Asia. Our own British or European otter *Lutra lutra lutra* is the nominate race and is generally accepted as occurring throughout Europe eastwards across Asia as far as China (where its place is taken by another sub-species), southwards to the Himalayas, in the Middle East and along the shores of Africa as far as Morocco and Algeria.

A wanderer by nature, the otter needs a large territory and on a lowland river of average size, 15–20 yards wide, a dog otter may require as much as 12½ miles for its home range. A bitch otter requires less space, up to 7 miles of river, so it is possible for more than one bitch to have her

Male European otter.

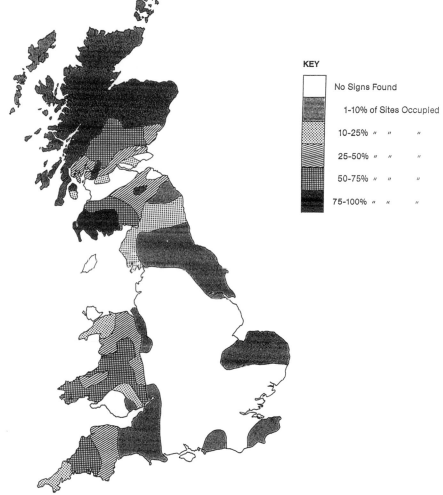

KEY

No Signs Found

1-10% of Sites Occupied

10-25% " " "

25-50% " " "

50-75% " " "

75-100% " " "

The approximate distribution of the otter in Britain 1986, showing the density of occupied sites in the various regions.

territory within the range of a single dog otter. Most of the work on which these measurements are based was carried out in Sweden (Erlinge, 1969). However, it seems likely that the otter's range may be larger in some areas of lowland Britain. In recent years extensive studies have been made on the movements and territoriality of otters in Britain, both by Don Jefferies and his colleagues of the Nature Conservancy Council and by Jim Green working for the Vincent Wildlife Trust. As a result of all this work, often involving radio tracking of wild otters, we now have a

• OTTER FACTS •

- As would be expected in animals of worldwide distribution, the different species of otter show considerable diversity. In size they range from the Asian short-clawed otter *Amblonyx cinerea*, which is around 30 inches (75cm) long, to the giant Brazilian otter *Pteronura brasiliensis*, which may grow to almost 9 feet (2.75m) in length.

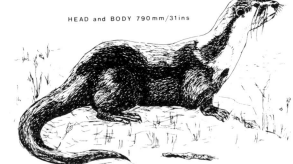

HEAD and BODY 790mm/31ins

- Individual otters vary in size, dogs being a good deal larger and heavier than bitches, with correspondingly broader heads and wider muzzles. A dog otter can measure up to 48 inches (120cm) or even more in length, and can weigh up to 30 pounds (14kg), although the average is probably nearer 24 pounds (11kg). A bitch may reach 28 pounds (12.3kg), with 16 pounds (7.4kg) a fair average.

Asian short-clawed otters hold their food in their forepaws when eating.

An otter's bed or couch in the middle of a reed bed.

far better idea of otters' territorial requirements. One thing is certain: the size of territory varies considerably according to the type of habitat and available food supply. An otter may need a much smaller territory under ideal conditions including maximum cover and food and minimum disturbance. But where conditions are not so suitable it may be forced to range further.

Bitch otters with young cubs are very aggressive, so it seems unlikely that the territories of two bitches would normally overlap. However, Bobby Tulloch, Warden for the Royal Society for the Protection of Birds in Shetland, has studied otters there and has observed two different and recognisable bitch otters using the same holt, although at different times. David Macdonald, working with foxes, has recently shown (in *Running With the Fox*, 1987) that these animals, previously thought to be solitary, sometimes live in social groups comprising one dog along with up to five adult vixens. He also made the astonishing discovery that some of these groups had territories averaging as little as 100 acres (45 hectares). While a dog otter may have two or even three bitches occupying their own territories within his range, it is most unlikely that the bitches would show any significant degree of tolerance towards each other, especially when protecting young cubs. However, as the cubs grow the bitches' aggressiveness declines, and this may account for several cases where two bitches with cubs have been seen to join up as a group, at least temporarily. The otter is a highly intelligent animal blessed with a considerable degree of individuality, so there will always be exceptions to every rule.

Otters mark their territories by depositing their droppings (spraint) at well defined places. The spraints themselves are usually loosely constructed and contain quantities of fish bones, scales, vertebrae and sometimes fur. Scent from the anal glands is passed with the droppings and serves to tell visiting otters the sex and status of the owner, its age, and how long ago it passed that way. An otter with a large territory may produce up to twenty spraints in a single night, so the quantity at each site is necessarily very small, but enough to establish the identity of the owner of the territory and to warn visiting otters to keep off. Spraints are usually deposited in prominent places such as the tops of boulders, on sand bars and ledges under bridges, on tussocks of grass or even on molehills. Sprainting is concentrated along commonly used highways where there is the best chance of a visiting otter coming across them.

The purpose of such marking is to avoid direct confrontation resulting in unnecessary and wasteful fighting. It simply warns passing otters that the territory is already occupied and that they must look elsewhere.

Otters living along undisturbed and remote stretches of seashore often have a much smaller territory, sometimes occupying little more than half a mile of shoreline. In such situations the boundaries between neighbouring territories are almost non-existent, and regular sprainting is often restricted to the area around the holt.

Spraint, a black tarry substance, is often difficult to find in deep vegetation.

Food and Feeding Habits

Otters are carnivores and live primarily upon fish, which may account for 70% or more of their diet, the remainder being made up of crayfish, frogs, birds and mammals. By examining stomach contents and analysing the remains of prey in the samples of spraint scientists have established the wide range of animal life upon which the otter feeds. As would be expected, diet varies according to the habitat and the availability of prey species.

Having dived with my tame otters when they were swimming completely free in the rivers of East Anglia, I am quite certain that they always go for the species which are easiest to catch. In addition to fish an otter will take river crayfish, whose flesh is sweet by human standards, and as they are small the otter sometimes devours the whole animal, crunching up the hard carapace and pincer claws. Birds up to the size of wild duck and moorhens are frequently taken. The latter appears to be

An otter's ungainly run.

Close-up of scales and teeth of a large fish, typical of the remains of an otter's kill.

the otter's favourite prey among birds, and one of the easiest for it to catch. I have seen my tame otters take them by underwater attack, pulling the moorhen under by a leg or pouncing on them in thick vegetation. I have seen several mallard which have been killed by wild otters, and on one occasion arrived on the scene only minutes after the attack and saw the duck lying dead on a spit of land jutting out into a lake. The promontory was heavily overgrown, and it took me some time to find a place to land from the rowing boat. When I did the mallard had disappeared, and all I found was a solitary otter print in the soft mud at the edge of the water. In my experience the otter usually eats only the breast of the duck, picking it clean. While it may do the same to a moorhen, it often devours much more of it.

Frogs are another favourite food item, and the otter enjoys playing with them rather as a cat plays with a mouse, pushing the wretched frog with its nose until it leaps, only to be prodded back into activity until the otter, tiring of the game, decides to eat it, holding the frog in its forepaws while chewing. Contrary to popular belief, the otter eats the entire frog and does not leave the skin turned neatly inside out as some writers have claimed. That is the work of rats, which deal with toads in the same manner. Rabbits and other small mammals also form part of the otter's diet, but I am sure that the small quantities of vegetable matter which have been found in otter's spraint were either eaten accidentally, perhaps when an otter was tearing up grass and sedge with its mouth in order to line its holt, or were present in the stomach of the otter's prey.

Otters have been reported feeding on carrion, and one or two keepers on the west coast of Scotland have told me that they were sure otters ate dead sheep or lambs when other food was scarce. Knowing from first-hand observation underwater how easy it is for an otter to catch fish, I cannot believe that it would waste time scouring the countryside for dead animals, and I know of no evidence to support the carrion-feeding belief. If otters regularly took carrion it would be a comparatively simple matter to study an individual's movements and hence its range by putting harmless dyes or small coloured plastic beads into carrion so that these would subsequently show up in the spraint.

• OTTER FACTS •

● The otter's skull is short, broad and flattened, with a well developed occipital region. The skull itself is thin and therefore vulnerable to blows. The jaw is short and powerful with an interlocking hinge and teeth which are adapted to crushing bones. A pair of long, curved canine teeth on each jaw help the otter to grip its prey, which it then chews with its large back teeth. The small pointed projections on these, the tubercles, cut through the flesh and grind the bones and other hard parts. As the otter's gullet is small the animal chews its food thoroughly and does not bolt it like a dog. On either side of the upper jaw are three incisors, one canine, four pre-molars and one molar. The lower jaw bears the same number of incisors and canines but three pre-molars and two molars. The bottom jaw moves only up and down motivated by powerful muscles which account for the otter's fearsome bite. (Aristotle is reputed to have said that an otter will bite and not let go until it hears the bone crush. Having lost part of the little finger of my right hand to an otter, I can vouch for the accuracy of this statement.) Both in captivity and in the wild otters are prone to tooth decay which sometimes sets up an infection. In captive otters this can usually be cured quite easily by a course of antibiotics, but otters in the wild are less fortunate.

A number of writers have claimed that otters eat freshwater mussels, but this has not been my experience. I have given captive otters both freshwater and saltwater mussels on a number of occasions over a considerable period of time, and they have never made any attempt to open the shells. Stephens (1957) fed freshwater mussels to her otters with the same results. However, if the shells are broken open the otter will eat the contents readily. The empty shells of freshwater mussels are frequently found lying on the bank, but they are the work of rats or coypu where these animals still exist. Both these rodents will dive in search of the molluscs, taking them on to the bank where they gnaw open the shells.

Otters living along the seashore have been observed to take a large variety of fish including butterfish, saithe, flounder and lumpfish, as well as lobsters and crabs. In the estuaries of Norfolk shore crabs, flounder and, in brackish water, sticklebacks have been recorded.

The weight of food eaten daily by an otter varies with the temperature of the air, the size of the otter and the type of food. Two of my captive European otters, both males, weighing 27 pounds (12.25kg) and 24 pounds (10.9kg) respectively, were fed their usual meat-mix and fresh whiting ad lib for a week. Both were used to eating this food and liked it. Their enclosures were rat-proof and any food uneaten overnight was collected and weighed every morning and the results deducted from the weight given. The larger animal consumed on average 3lb 4oz (1.5kg) per day and the smaller 3lb 1oz (1.4kg) per day. Captive otters consume more food in cold weather, and these tests were carried out during the winter with an average daily temperature of 32°F (0°C). It is likely that an otter in the wild requires more food because of the energy needed to hunt successfully. On the other hand wild otters are rarely faced with a surfeit.

Small fish like sticklebacks are eaten while the otter swims at the surface, but larger specimens are taken ashore to be consumed and some bones and scales may be left. In the case of cyprinids the fish's pharangeal teeth are usually left on the bank surrounded by a patch of scales, and it is then possible to identify the quarry by the teeth.

Otters have a relatively rapid and incomplete digestion which results in many small bones and scales being present in their spraint. These and other fragments can be examined either with the naked eye or under a binocular microscope.

If an otter kills a large fish, as sometimes happens with salmon that are weak from spawning, or large carp, it may eat only the flesh from part of the victim. When this happens little of value is likely to show up in the spraint. Some authors have claimed that otters will eat eggs, but whole eggs given to my captive otters were either ignored or used briefly as playthings. Only if I broke the egg open would they lick up the contents.

The otter's preference for fish has in the past frequently brought it into conflict with anglers, and in medieval times when large numbers of fish were kept for food in small stewponds raiding otters were regarded as pests and killed by every possible means. Nowadays I am glad to say that few anglers consider the otter a pest, and even on the more exclusive trout rivers most would consider an evening's fishing enhanced by the rare glimpse of an otter going about its night's hunting. That this is so is borne out by the number of requests we have had from landowners wanting us to reintroduce otters on their trout streams. The otter's large range and its habit of remaining in one locality for only a night or two at a time ensure that it does not overfish a particular stretch of river. Fish farms, where large concentrations of fish are held in very small pools, are another matter, but these can and should be fenced against otters and other predators. More recently a rather similar situation has developed where comparatively small lakes such as gravel pits are heavily stocked with large specimen fish, usually carp, for sport fishing. An otter coming across such a haven of unlimited delicacies would be foolish not to take advantage of it, but such concentrations of fish are, like the medieval stewpond, quite unnatural, and their owners would be wise to take the precaution of fencing them against all predators. Nor would the expense be prohibitive now that it is possible to buy plastic rabbit fencing complete with a built-in electric circuit. Although little over 2 feet in height such a fence would be most effective in excluding otters, besides being light and quickly erected. An otter approaching such a fence would

An Asian short-clawed otter standing for food.

almost certainly receive a sharp shock on its nose, enough to deter it without doing it any harm. The one problem with such a fence is that the lowest electrified wire is only a few inches above ground-level, which means that the grass and other vegetation must be kept cut at all times to prevent an electrical short back to earth.

29

• OTTER FACTS •

- The shape and hairiness of an otter's nose is different in every species and is a useful criterion for classification. In the common otter the hairless black portion or rhinarium is smaller than in most species and has a characteristic shape rather like a very shallow W.

- Belonging to a group of animals known as mustelids or *Mustelidae*, otters are related to stoats, weasels, polecats, mink, martens, and even to wolverines, skunks and badgers. All of these creatures have one thing in common, powerful scent glands which are embedded in the muscle of the anal region. In the European otter these two glands are about the size of cherries and are found in both dog and bitch otters. Their main function is to produce a strong-smelling brown oily liquid which enters the anus through two small tubes. This oil is deposited on various objects to mark the otter's territory. A sudden shock will also stimulate the glands to release this noxious fluid which, in the case of cubs, is milky-white rather than brown.

- Dog otters have an *os penis* or *bacculum*. This is a bone which supports the penis and is found only in certain mammals. Penile bones used to be coveted by otter hunters and were frequently made into tie-pins. This bone varies in size and the largest measured by Marie Stephens (1957) was more than 2½ inches (6cm) long and ⅜ of an inch (1cm) in diameter. That this bone is often damaged or broken is confirmed by Stephens, who examined a number of dead otters. It is commonly believed that the damage is done when rival males fight, but there is a lack of reliable evidence to support this, and in any case penile bones are quite fragile and are prone to fracture under natural conditions including, I suspect, during mating.

CHAPTER 3

World Beneath the Water

An otter in a weir pool – a favourite place to hunt for fish.

British otter swimming in the tail of the mill race.

It was one of those rare, brilliant June days, the sun shining from a cloudless sky, as I stood on the bridge at the head of the millpool looking down into the sparkling clear water. I could see stones on the bottom and the waving beds of water-moss bowing and swaying to the current. As I struggled into my wetsuit and a friend lifted the heavy weight of the air cylinder on to my back one of our tame otters, Fury, was already enjoying the pool, searching for crayfish in the stony shallows. Clad in flippers and a facemask I plodded awkwardly out through the shallows into the deep waters of the millrace, where I was able to slide beneath the surface into the murky depths of the pool. To human ears the silence of the underwater world is broken only by the rasping and bubbling noises of one's breathing equipment. Distances have gone, for it is rarely possible to see more than a few feet, and a human diver lying on the bottom of the river and looking upwards can see nothing on land or in the air, however clear the water. All he sees is a silvery opaque sheet like frosted glass. On that day visibility was a bare yard and I frequently bumped into unseen objects. Fury thought the whole business was great fun and kept materialising out of the murk to peer into my facemask. Sometimes I found myself struggling through almost impenetrable tangles of pondweed, and the only fish I saw were shoals of fry which scattered and quickly disappeared into the greyness. At first I found the underwater world baffling and sometimes rather sinister, but gradually the way between the patches of weed became as familiar as a well-known woodland path. In the shallows the sun flickered on the bright green crinkled beds of waterlilies, whose submerged leaves are cabbage-like and often dusted by a fine layer of silt. Fish showed up well against such a pale background and clusters of small fry, minnows, sticklebacks and rudd hung suspended in the clear water. At my approach they darted this way and that flashing sparks of silver and green. The sun sent prongs of light stabbing into the depths ahead of me, as though emanating from a light source on my head, but if a cloud obscured the sun visibility dropped like a winter fog. In the deeper reaches the sun sent shimmering bars of golden light across the pale mud where emerald green spikelets of the introduced Canadian pondweed grew as close as a lawn. In open patches small speckled gudgeon hugged the bottom, beautifully camouflaged against the mud and gravel, their protruding mouths wide open to suck in insect larvae and other minute forms of animal life carried to them by the lazy current. Above them the floating leaves of arrowhead and waterlilies lay silhouetted against the opaque ceiling of the river, anchored to the bottom by long ropes of brown tendrils through which swam shoals of silvery fish. An avenue between the swaying stems of shining pondweed led to an underwater garden rich in vegetation surrounding an amphitheatre of pale yellow sand. Fish of all sizes swam at every depth, shoals of perch moving gently amongst the forest of stalks, their grey-green bodies striped vertically to match the translucent leaves of the pondweed. Often I followed Fury along the paths between the beds of waterweed. Fish were everywhere, and

An otter lying on the surface of the water, filmed from below.

A British otter lying beneath the surface looks down at the photographer.

looking down into the deep water I often saw the dark thick-bodied forms of fat tench passing beneath me, keeping close to the floor of the river. It was on expeditions such as these that I was able to enter the truly secret part of an otter's life, and to see at first hand how perfectly adapted it was to this silent underwater environment where it moved with effortless grace so that the pursuit and capture of a fish usually took no more than a few brief seconds. Gradually I came to understand how it was that an otter caught its prey so easily.

If a fish looks upward through the water it can see objects on land or in the air, but only if they are within an angle of about 98°. In effect the fish has a round skylight above its head, and outside the area covered by this 'bubble' the watery surface reflects the light and the fish sees only a mirror picture of the bottom of the river. Sight is extremely important to most fish, and they can see over a field of about 330° horizontally, their clearest vision being straight ahead, where a field within an angle of about 30° is covered by both eyes. In addition to excellent sight many fish have keen hearing and a well-developed sense of smell. They also have a sense of taste located in the mouth, on the underside of the head and spread over part of the body surface. In addition to these senses the fish has a lateral line running along each side of its body. It comprises a series of sense organs, small open tubes, connected by a duct filled with slime. The lateral line organs enable the fish to estimate very accurately the direction and distance of any disturbance in the water which sets up pressure waves. The fish can 'feel' the presence of other fish, waterplants, stones, or any object which enters its field of sensitivity. All this may sound as though it is well equipped to avoid an approaching predator. However, it suffers from two serious drawbacks. Firstly, it cannot see an object immediately beneath it at all distinctly, so an otter swimming along the bottom is often able to curve gracefully upwards and grab a fish from below without even the beginning of a chase. Secondly, while game fish such as salmon and trout can move exceedingly quickly over long distances, coarse fish such as roach, rudd, tench and chubb, which form the bulk of an otter's diet, are slow swimmers and poor stayers, often diving into the nearest bed of reed, hiding their heads but leaving their tails waving in the current, asking to be winkled out by a passing otter. Nor does an otter have any problem with eels, since they often attempt to escape by hiding beneath a stone or in a tangle of thick weed where the otter's sensitive vibrissae – its whiskers – quickly locate its quarry.

When swimming on the surface the otter dog-paddles with all four feet, using its tail as a rudder. It is unable to attain much speed, but is able to listen and look around. Underwater the otter tucks its forepaws back close to its flanks and drives itself forward by a powerful flexing action of its rear quarters and rudder. The hind paws may be kicked occasionally for added impetus, but the main drive comes from the otter's body and rudder, much as a whale uses its massive tail flukes in powerful vertical strokes. The otter's action beneath the surface can best be described as undulating and apparently effortless, but its speed is considerable – up to 7–9mph, or more in short bursts – and I could never keep up with any of my tame otters however hard I tried. Like humans, otters have positive buoyancy and rise to the surface if they stop swimming. This enables an otter to lie on the surface with its head under water, watching all that goes on below. Since an otter swims faster and more easily underwater its normal method of travelling consists of a series of shallow dives, surfacing regularly to breathe. The dive is effected by dipping its head below the surface and at the same time flexing its body and driving itself down by two or three powerful kicks of its webbed hind feet. The action is so smooth the animal seems to slide downwards. A human diver attempting

A dog otter at the start of a dive.

the same manoeuvre is taught to attempt to touch his toes, as it were, thus forcing his head vertically downwards, and with propulsion provided by his flippers a diver can drive himself down into the depths, though not, I'm afraid, with anything like the grace of an otter. When an otter intends to dive deep it rolls over in a graceful curve, its rudder following its body in a perfect arc. The action is porpoise-like and gives an impression of great power, the body almost doubling up at the start of the dive. Seen from below, the otter plummets down, air bubbles streaming behind. Sometimes an otter will tread water with its hind paws, its body almost vertical, so that it can raise its head and neck as high as possible for better vision. From this position the animal can apparently sink beneath the surface, leaving scarcely a ripple. Seen from below the action differs little from a normal dive, except that the head is drawn under before the body is flexed and the hind paws kicked to provide the downward propulsion. If alarmed when swimming on the surface, the otter can crash dive instantly, with a mighty splash caused by the rudder hitting the water. Two otters at play, especially a courting pair, will occasionally leap completely clear of the water, often several times in quick succession, like dolphins. To do this they put on a tremendous burst of speed in order to provide the momentum to keep the movement going.

A valvular action automatically closes the otter's nostrils on submersion, enabling it to drink with its head completely underwater, although it is also capable of lapping daintily like a cat. When Jeanne was rearing our two young British otters, Kate and Lucy, she used to hold them on her lap, letting them plunge their heads into a firmly-held mug to suck up the water with mighty gurgles. This they would do quite happily until they had quenched their thirst, when Lucy in particular would sometimes withdraw her head and blow out hard, spraying everyone in the kitchen with ice-cold droplets.

The otter's small rounded ears offer little resistance to water flow, and have the same reflex response as the nostrils. Small flaps of furred skin which make up the ear pinnae close over the openings as soon as the water rises over them.

A quick turn under water to catch a fish.

The eyes of otters are upturned and small, and on land their sight is rather poor. But beneath the water their vision is remarkably good.

Despite having lungs of large air capacity, the left with two lobes and the right with four, otters cannot remain underwater for more than one or two minutes, and dives are usually limited to less than 50 seconds, with over one minute being very exceptional. They occasionally descend to considerable depth, and there is a record of a North American otter being drowned in a crab pot which was set in water 60 feet deep (Scheffer, 1953).

Otters are impervious to temperatures close to freezing owing to their thick, water-repellent coat and their layer of subcutaneous fat. The secret of an otter's coat, which has long been coveted by man for his own use, is that it consists of an underlayer of very dense, waterproof fur like the close pile of a carpet, protected by an outer covering of longer and stiffer guard hairs. When the animal dives, air is trapped between the two layers, providing further insulation. The pressure of water forces the air out in the characteristic chain of bubbles. When diving with my tame otters I have noticed that bubbles of air also leave the corners of the mouth and, curling upwards, unite with those from the fur so that a continual stream is forced back along the otter's body, rising to the surface from the area around the base of the tail. Such fine fur has to be kept in immaculate condition if it is to remain waterproof, and otters spend a great deal of their time on land rolling and rubbing themselves dry and grooming their coats. They do this with a clipper-like nibbling motion of their incisor teeth. As soon as an otter leaves the water its coat breaks into an irregular spiky pattern caused by the outer guard hairs sticking together. If forced to remain too long in the water an otter gradually becomes sodden, waterlogged and cold. This can result in death by exposure and no doubt accounted for so many half-drowned otters being killed by hounds in the days when otter-hunting was still legal.

I have often watched one of my tame otters catch a fish, sometimes within a few inches of my facemask. I have had eels chased by an otter attempt to use my body as a refuge, something which always sends cold shivers down my back as I have a horror of eels, especially large ones, though curiously I do not mind snakes as long as I know when to expect them. Pursued by an otter an eel can put on quite a turn of speed, no longer swimming with its rather slow, sinuous movement, but fleeing straight as an arrow, the lateral waggle of its tail speeded up to a blur of movement. Seen from the same level the eel looks more like a silvery-green fish and less like a watersnake. Sometimes the otter took its quarry in its forepaws, at the same time biting it, and surfacing with a fish in its mouth, but most prey was seized in the otter's jaws. When pursuing a fish underwater an otter can turn with remarkable agility using its rudder and its webbed feet. Eels often seem to stimulate an otter to play, and I have watched mine on many occasions release an eel they have just caught, allowing it to swim away only to be recaptured time and again.

My tame otters often swam very close to the bottom of the river so that they could attack a fish from below, thus achieving the advantage of surprise. Observed from above the fish in a shoal appear to lie one behind the other, but seen from the same level it immediately becomes

The otter rises to the surface with the fish clasped to its chest. At the surface it will take the fish in its mouth.

Eels are an otter's favourite diet.

apparent that each individual, while conforming to the general pattern, adjusts its depth and distance to keep clear of its neighbour's wash or slipstream. At the approach of an otter the shoal invariably scatters, the victim apparently chosen at the last minute fleeing for the nearest cover. Almost at once the remaining fish reassemble as though they know that the danger for them has passed. Herds of antelope can react in the same way to an attack by lions.

Moving water nearly always stimulates an otter to play, and in the millpool I always made a point of swimming along the bottom to the deepest part immediately beneath the old red-brick road bridge where an arched culvert ran back to the sluice gate operated from within the mill itself. The water roared down the dark culvert, tumbling over the sill and into the pool in a torrent of creamy white froth. Down below visibility was almost nil, but by lying to one side of the main current, a favourite place for the fish which live in the pool, and looking upwards, I could watch the vortex of brilliant white cloud formed by a myriad of silver bubbles where the entire volume of the river crashed down into the deeps, rolling over and over as it dashed past me, small strings of bubbles flying off the mainstream like puffs of white smoke. This sparkling turmoil was the otters' favourite place and I always marvelled at their ability to master the torrent. I have seen them dive straight down, flashing past me, body spinning in an explosion of bubbles. Often an otter will approach the roughest water from below, driving itself upward through the swirling cloud to surface below the sill, only to turn and dive again allowing the force of the current to toss it downstream like a piece of driftwood. In the clear shallows an otter would often search for crayfish, turning over stones the size of bricks by forcing its muzzle beneath one side then heaving with its head while kicking powerfully with its hind feet. Sometimes it found a round pebble an appealing plaything. Then it would turn on its back close to the bottom of the river and juggle the stone between its forepaws and chest. Often it lost interest before surfacing, at other times it would swim up with the stone in its paws and continue to play on the surface, dropping it and diving down to catch it again.

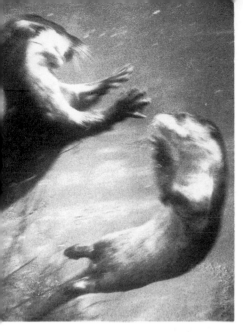

Much of the otter's courtship takes the form of play and mock fights both on land and in the water, sometimes above but often below the surface, and I have often watched two young otters indulging in such play, diving in pursuit of one another, rolling and spinning as one animal, shadow-boxing together as if floating in space, all the time surrounded by a halo of silver bubbles. When the chase took them upwards I watched them burst through the bright ceiling of the river as they disappeared into the world of sunshine leaving behind them a cloud of spent bubbles drifting on the current.

Breeding habits

The European or British otter is not easy to breed in captivity, and as far as is known no European otters were successfully bred, certainly in Britain, between that recorded by A. H. Cox in 1881 and 1970 when the species was bred at the Norfolk Wildlife Park for the first time. Since then I have of course bred British otters regularly every year, both at the Park and, more recently, at the Otter Trust. This has enabled me to spend many hours watching the family life of the otter from shortly after the birth of cubs until they were weaned four months later. As a result I have been able to accumulate a great deal of hitherto unrecorded data, for it is to captive otters that we must turn for information of this kind since an otter in the wild spends so much of its time either below ground, in the safety of its holt, or fishing in the inaccessible depths of a river, usually at night.

Two British otters playing under water.

Play like this is often part of courtship.

When I first hit upon the idea of recording the life of an otter from virtually the day it was born I provided one of my tamer bitch otters with an artificial holt, the back of which consisted of a plate-glass window built into the end of a light-tight wooden hut. A photo floodlamp controlled by a rheostat so that the illumination could be increased slowly enabled me to watch and film a complete record of events within the holt from the time the cubs were four days old. At birth otter cubs are about 5 inches (12cm) long, including their tails, and are covered with short, pale grey fur. Their eyes are closed and their square-shaped muzzles, small orifices

A litter of British otters at the Otter Trust.

and pads are bright salmon pink. The bitch curls her body tightly around them, often sleeping with her chin resting on the base of her rudder. Whenever she moves the cubs chirp like small birds. Bitch otters have four teats and at first the cubs suckle every three to four hours. When hungry they struggle upwards through the fur of the bitch's belly searching for her teats, twittering softly until they find them. They suckle vigorously, wagging their little tails from side to side and kneading the bitch's stomach with their forepaws. Each bout of feeding lasts from ten to fifteen minutes and sometimes a cub will go to sleep still holding the teat in its mouth. After they are fed the bitch takes each cub in turn holding it on its back between her forepaws while she licks its anal region. This not only keeps the cub clean but stimulates it to defecate which it does with much tail-wagging, the bitch licking up the faeces as they are voided.

For the first two weeks the cubs can scarcely crawl. Their eyes do not open until they are thirty to thirty-five days old, and by this time they can crawl but not walk properly and are able to hold up their heads.

The colour of their fur slowly changes to a darker grey becoming brown as they get older while the interval between bouts of suckling gradually increases. During this period the bitch otter spends almost all her time lying with her cubs, leaving them during the night only long enough to feed herself. When one month old an otter cub weighs between 1lb 9oz (700g) and 1lb 12oz (800g) depending on its sex, increasing to between 2lb 6oz (1075g) and 2lb 12oz (1250g) by the time it is two months old.

At about seven weeks of age the cubs suddenly begin to develop more rapidly, and by this time they can run although their balance is poor and their legs still weak. They also begin to eat solid food, usually fish which the bitch brings to them. As soon as they are eating properly their faeces change in form and the bitch no longer licks them up. Instead the cubs begin to leave the holt to defecate a short distance away.

By the time they are ten weeks old the cubs are eating well and are much stronger on their legs. They still suckle the bitch and continue to do so until at least fourteen weeks old, but before then, usually at about

Four-week-old cubs nestle into their mother's flank.

A female otter licks her cub's anal region to stimulate defecation.

three months or a few days earlier, they take their first swim. Much has been written on this subject, usually stressing the point that a bitch otter has to teach, even coerce, her cubs to swim. I have watched cubs taking to the water for the first time on many occasions and there appear to be considerable individual differences in behaviour, not only among the cubs but between individual cubs as well as individual bitch otters. I recall one bitch which had two cubs, one of which, a male, was very precocious and kept running to the water's edge only to be hauled out by the scruff of its neck, and the other, a female, much more timid, spending most of her time skulking in a clump of rushes until eventually her mother hauled her out by the scruff of her neck and dragged her into the water. The cub swam at once, dog-paddling rather unsteadily, but thereafter it needed no persuasion to leave dry land. On another occasion I watched a bitch otter bring her litter of three cubs down to the edge of their pool at dusk. Slipping into the water herself the bitch otter swam slowly along the edge of the bank and after some hesitation, running up and down, two of the cubs decided to follow her swimming in the curiously unco-ordinated way of all very young cubs, their bodies bobbing along like corks. The third cub, lacking the courage to take the plunge, ran up and down at the water's edge squeaking until its siblings returned. Having watched similar incidents on a number of occasions I am sure bitch otters often encourage their cubs to swim and sometimes even go as far as dragging them into the water, but I do not believe this is the general rule. In the wild a bitch otter disturbed while her cubs are still too young to swim will carry them to safety in her mouth, one at a time. An observer seeing this may have mistakenly assumed that she was dragging her cub into the water in order to teach it to swim. On the other hand during a June heatwave with the midday temperature around 27°C (80°F) I watched a captive bitch bring a month-old cub out of her holt carrying it in her mouth to the edge of a pool where she dunked it several times before taking it back again – presumably to cool it down and to prevent it becoming dehydrated from the heat.

By the time the cubs are four months old they follow the bitch on her fishing expeditions and soon learn to catch their own quarry. In the wild their life of wandering has begun, since by this time the bitch will frequently have moved her family to a different holt. Although otters see very well underwater in clear conditions, they are somewhat myopic on land, and young cubs have very limited vision when their eyes first open, being unable to recognise objects more than 3 or 4 yards away until they are nearly three months old. Thereafter their sight improves rapidly, and our tame otter cubs were able to distinguish Jeanne or me from a stranger at a distance of at least 20 yards by the time they were four months old. As might be expected of an animal with such sensitive ears, otter cubs rely a great deal on hearing to keep in contact with each other or with their mother, both adult and young using those familiar very high-pitched squeaks often referred to as a whistle. I have frequently observed my tame otters picking up and reacting to a sound which was totally inaudible to human ears, as if they were receiving it on a different wavelength. Next to hearing, the otter's vibrissae may well provide the

Eurasian otter and cubs in their holt.

most important sense, certainly when the otter is hunting. The long, stiff whiskers are tactile and highly sensitive, being set in large nerve pads on each side of the snout with two or more clumps set further back below the chin on each side. In addition there are one or two whiskers on the face between the eye and the ear and on the 'elbow' of each foreleg.

Not much is known about the dog otter's relationship with the family, and as we make a point of removing the dog otter before the bitch gives birth in order to leave her to rear her cubs in peace captive breeding has not taught us much about this aspect of otter breeding behaviour. However, on several occasions when we were unaware that a bitch was pregnant the dog otter has been left with her until after the birth of her cubs, and in no case did he interfere either with the bitch or the cubs. From the many first-hand accounts of pairs of otters being seen in the wild with young cubs in attendance it seems certain that the dog may accompany the family from time to time, though possibly for only a day or two at a stretch. There is no evidence, as far as I know, that the dog otter takes food either to the bitch or to the cubs, and on the one occasion when we left a dog otter in a large enclosure with the bitch and her cubs he made no attempt to take food to them although he was seen to visit the holt. Bitch otters with young cubs are very protective towards them, and the male almost certainly keeps his distance until the cubs are well grown and the bitch less likely to attack him.

The cubs stay with their mother until they are about one year old, although in the last two or three months of this period they become increasingly independent. When they finally leave her they probably stay fairly close to the home territory for some time before wandering away on their own. This is likely to be the most vulnerable time in an otter's life, since it is exposed to numerous dangers and is compelled to range far and wide through unfamiliar country while establishing its own territory. This may mean journeying to a different river or to a distant part of the coastline, since favourable territories are likely to be occupied by resident otters always ready to drive away intruders.

The comparatively long period during which otter cubs are dependent on their mother means that a bitch can rear only one litter in a year, and

in practice there is usually a longer interval between successive litters.

A bitch otter is believed to come into oestrus every forty to forty-five days and to remain so for about fourteen days. It is during this time that her increased scent, carried on the current and concentrated at her sprainting places, attracts the dog otter, which soon picks up the unmistakable sign and so the two animals come together. The bitch may not be ready to mate but the dog will keep trying until he succeeds. I have often watched courtship leading to mating in captive otters, and it nearly always starts with the bitch chittering in a manner indicating that she is likely to become aggressive if she is approached too closely by the dog, but after a time she chitters less and may even approach the male or chase him, in which case the dog invariably runs away. Both animals spraint and scent mark at various places. After a time the dog otter begins to approach the bitch, sometimes getting quite close only to retreat when she lunges at him. Should the bitch otter lie and roll in the grass the dog will sometimes rush in and roll against her on his side only to jump away, often right over her, before she can bite him. When doing this he moves his rudder very vigorously from side to side in a pronounced scything action. After several hours of this kind of play the bitch usually chitters less and begins bouts of exaggerated, even frenetic, rolling and drying movements in the grass, often lying on her back and waving her front paws in the air. Thus the two otters gradually come together and now begins a period of chasing each other in the water, usually without making a direct approach, each sheering away at the last minute. As time goes on they lose their fear of each other and settle down to a period of normal play including chasing and mock fights. Mating may take place soon after the animals are put together, or may be delayed for several weeks, but copulation always takes place in the water and is preceded by vigorous play, the dog chasing the bitch in and out of the pool and all over their large enclosure. At times both otters swim and dive together, twisting and corkscrewing through the water, and there is also a great deal of mock fighting, the pair facing each other submerged except for their heads and lunging at each other's faces and necks. Finally the bitch lies still on the surface, her back awash and her rudder arched and held just clear of the water. The dog mounts her from behind, grasping her loins between his forepaws and gripping the back of her neck in his mouth. Copulation lasts around fifteen to twenty-five minutes, the pair rolling over and over sideways and sometimes disappearing below the surface. Quite short bursts of vigorous pelvic thrusts by the dog otter are separated by longer periods of rest or less vigorous thrusting. Throughout copulation the dog otter maintains his grip on the back of the bitch's neck, frequently forcing her head beneath the water.

The gestation period of the European otter is sixty-three days plus or minus three days, and shortly before the cubs are born the bitch often brings considerable quantities of fresh vegetation into the holt making a bulky nest with a hollow in the centre where she lies.

From one to four cubs may be born in a litter though as many as four is a rarity and has occurred only three times at the Otter Trust where, up to the end of 1988, 89 European otter cubs have been born and reared from 53 litters giving an average of 1.7 cubs reared per litter. During the same period 28 cubs were born and reared in the Norfolk Wildlife Park from 16 litters giving an average of 1.75 cubs reared per litter. Bitch otters have no specific breeding season, so cubs may be born in any month of the year, though from records kept at the Otter Trust there seems to be a peak in the autumn and early winter.

Bitch otters are able to breed in their third year, and possibly as early as two years old, while some dog otters mature earlier, and I have recorded a young male only eighteen months old when he fathered cubs. The youngest of our bitch otters to breed was two years and two months old when her first litter was born, while the oldest was over five.

Both dog and bitch otters will line their holts with grass, reeds, waterplants or other vegetation which they tear up and carry in their mouths, but bitch otters usually make a more substantial bed. Both sexes often incorporate quite thick twigs 15mm or more in diameter, which might appear to make the bed uncomfortable, but such bulky material may ensure better air circulation and therefore a drier bed. On the other hand otters do not appear to seek out dry vegetation, and very often the bed is decidedly damp. Should the entrance to the holt be underwater the bedding will naturally get sodden on the way in, as it will if the otter has to swim to reach its holt.

An otter always has a number of holts scattered throughout its territory. Some of these may consist of burrows in the banks of the river, often amongst the roots of riverside trees, others of small caves or cavities amongst rocks or even hollows beneath piles of branches or other debris. Occasionally an otter will make a nest of reeds within the seclusion of a large reedbed. Some writers have suggested that, in order to encourage otters, elaborate artificial holts consisting of drainpipes leading into a concrete chamber beneath the ground should be constructed, preferably with one entrance near the water's edge and another further back on dry ground.

Although the provision of such artificial holts is rarely necessary, a simpler shelter in the form of piles of logs set above ground with a space or compartment in the middle will often be used by otters for a day or two's shelter. Such stick piles should be substantial in order to make the interior dark and keep out the weather, but they have the advantage of being cheap and easy to build. Furthermore a number of such shelters constructed at suitable points throughout an otter's territory would be far better than one or two of the more expensive and elaborate permanent holts. Otters will often use naturally occurring piles of sticks and other debris as a temporary shelter.

Communication

'Social' otters – species in which the male and female can remain together throughout their lives, like the Asian short-clawed otter or the Indian smooth-coated otter *Lutra (Lutrogale) perspicilata* – have an extensive vocabulary or range of sounds which they require in order to maintain the cohesion of the family group when travelling or hunting in a band.

The European otter is by comparison a silent animal, which is to be expected since, being solitary by nature, it does not as a rule have or need such an extensive vocabulary. The best known otter noise is the so-called whistle, which is not a whistle at all but a high-pitched and piercing squeak. That it is the most familiar vocalisation is due not only to the prominence given it by numerous writers, but also to the fact that it is the sound most likely to be heard by the casual observer. Young cubs are able to call loudly in this way by the time they are two months old. It is a contact call and means roughly 'I'm here, where are you?' A pair of otters keep in contact this way, and cubs use it constantly whenever they become separated from the rest of the litter or from their mother. A bitch otter who has lost a cub will keep calling all the time she is searching for it.

However, by far the commonest sound made by otters is the 'hah', a short, explosive exhalation. Unlike the contact call this sound does not carry far and is used in various ways, although it is basically an alarm call or a question mark. A bitch otter uses it to make her cubs hide when danger threatens. An otter approaching an unfamiliar object drawn on by its curiosity will keep moving a few steps forward, stopping to 'hah' before retreating a few paces until it overcomes its fear.

Young cubs 'chirrup' like small birds. At first the sound is barely audible, but gradually, as the cubs grow, it turns into a louder squeak which eventually develops into the high-pitched contact call.

The otter's threat call is a querulous chittering noise on a rising note. If this does not have the desired effect it turns into a scream of rage just before the animal attacks its adversary. A similar noise, though deeper in tone and quieter, indicates the same warning but of lower intensity, rather like the difference between a dog growling quietly and snarling. The lower note is frequently made by a bitch otter when the dog begins his advances during courtship.

When a pair of otters are reunited after a period of separation they will greet each other by briefly touching noses while uttering a low 'whicker-ing' – rather like the noise made by badgers in similar circumstances. It is quiet, friendly and confidential.

Although the facial expression of an otter does not change much, the animal is capable of other visual signals indicating its mood. The scything action of the rudder from side to side in the face of attack from the rear has already been mentioned and is most frequently seen when one otter has food and is afraid another otter may attempt to steal it. The scything

A twist of grass made by a bitch otter in captivity. Similar twists are made in the wild but the precise meaning of this behaviour is unknown.

of the rudder is then an attempt to push away the adversary advancing from behind.

The opening of the mouth displaying the teeth while chittering with anger reinforces the threat of aggression. On the other hand an otter in a friendly mood, especially during pre-courtship play, will often roll over on to its back and paw the air with its forefeet held close together.

The otter's external ears may be small, but they are quite expressive and are constantly on the move, being pricked forward when the animal is listening intently and laid back when it is angry. It seems likely that in a solitary and far-ranging animal like the otter the olfactory sense plays a major part in communication between individuals. The importance of regular sprainting sites has already been mentioned, and no doubt the anal scent glands play a major part in this means of communication.

Bitch otters sometimes produce a white, opaque, jelly-like substance which has a strong musky odour. It may be deposited on top of spraint or quite separately and I have found it in the wild as well as in our otter enclosures. Its significance is not yet fully understood, but it appears to be produced when a bitch is in oestrus, a fact doubtless well known to dog otters. Otters also make sign heaps of twists of grass on which jelly or spraint may be deposited. The precise meaning of this behaviour is being studied by scientists, and it is not known for certain whether it can be attributed to only one or to both sexes. We once found a twist of grass made by one of our captive bitch otters, and it seems likely that the practice, like the production of anal jelly, is associated with oestrus and may be a means of making the signs more conspicuous.

Dog otters are thought to produce a similar jelly which is usually dark in colour.

Mortality

To find a dead otter is a fairly rare event, and with the cessation of otter hunting and the granting of total protection to the species under the Wild Life and Countryside Act of 1981 one might hope that deaths at the hand of man would have become less frequent. However, this is not necessarily so, as Paul Chanin showed in 1985. Statistics compiled during the

OTTER DEATHS IN ENGLAND

	(%)
Killed on roads	34
Killed deliberately	37
Found dead	16
Caught in fish traps	10
Killed by dogs	2
Other causes	1
Number of otters	165

Note: Other causes include electrocution and drowning under ice.
(From Paul Chanin, *The Natural History of Otters*, Croom Helm, 1985)

The corpse of an otter from which the skin has been removed by fishermen using fyke nets to catch eels.

1970s, when he collected information on the deaths of 165 otters in England, reveal that more than three-quarters had been killed deliberately or inadvertently by man.

It is to be hoped that increasing public awareness, and a general swing by country people to the idea that the otter is not a predator of fish to be destroyed, but a seriously threatened animal which needs protecting if it is not to become extinct, may result in fewer otters being killed deliberately, especially in lowland England where the animal has now become so rare. Like badgers, otters have well-defined traditional routes or paths, and this accounts for the fact that certain sections of road have become otter blackspots simply because an important otter path or highway happens to cross a road in that particular place so that, over a period of years, several individuals may be run over. The increase in the use of fyke nets for eel fishing also poses a serious threat, particularly in lowland Britain on the slow, sluggish rivers much loved by otters where eels abound. Fyke nets are long tubular nets 6 feet or more in length, ending with a bag or cod end. The entrance to the net is held open by a hoop varying in diameter from 2 feet across to 3 feet or more. Inside the body of the net are two or more hoops each supporting a cone-shaped funnel of netting, the end one terminating at the entrance to the bag or cod end. These funnels effectively prevent the escape of any eel that has entered the trap. Unfortunately the outer two funnels are large enough for an otter to pass through with comparative ease, and once inside it is quite impossible for the animal to escape and it quickly drowns. The nets are sometimes set singly or as a pair facing each other, the space between being filled by a 'leader' – a vertical wall of netting around 65 feet long to guide the eels into one or other of the fyke tunnels. Sometimes the nets are set in fleets of thirty or more with leaders anchored in the water in such a way as to guide fish into the entrance of each net. Fyke nets, particularly when set in numbers, are lethal to otters who, intensely curious by nature and possibly attracted by fish inside the nets, are almost certain to enter them and drown. Such nets if used regularly could soon wipe out the otter population of any river especially when numbers are low.

If public opinion can be enlisted, the government might eventually be persuaded to pass legislation enforcing the fixing of large mesh grids or otter excluders over the entrance to all fyke nets. Such excluders might consist of a metal grid with a mesh of $3\frac{1}{2}$ inches square, which would not prevent the entry of the largest eel but would effectively exclude otters. Nor would these excluders be difficult or expensive to fit. More of a problem are crab and lobster pots, since although the largest eel will slip easily through a $3\frac{1}{2}$-inch square grid, which would exclude an otter, the same is not true of a large crab or lobster. On the other hand, inshore fishing for crabs and lobsters takes place on rocky, uninhabited shores, particularly on the west coast of Scotland where there is a healthy otter population better able to withstand this increasing hazard. It has been suggested that the problem might be overcome by making the entrance to the crab or lobster pot oval instead of round, with the maximum width, while sufficient to admit a large crab or lobster, too narrow for an otter to squeeze through. Experiments will have to be carried out to see whether this is a practical idea. If it is, there will then follow the difficult task of persuading fishermen that such an innovation would not result in any reduction of their catches.

CHAPTER 4

The Formation of the Otter Trust

According to the naturalist Millais, otters were so abundant on the river Yare in Norfolk in 1557 that the Norwich Assembly passed a law compelling every fisherman in the area to keep a dog to hunt them. Failure to do so would lead to a fine of ten shillings, a huge sum in those days. Not many years later central government passed an Act for the Preservation of Grayne which allowed parish constables and church wardens to pay bounties for the heads of a number of wild animals believed to be destructive to man's interests. These included hedgehogs, weasels, stoats, badgers, foxes and otters. In the case of the otter the bounty varied from sixpence to one shilling per head. Every conceivable device was used to hunt them, including traps, guns and dogs, and the improvement of firearms during the eighteenth century may well have contributed to the start of the otter's long and steady decline in this country, for by the end of that century the great artist and naturalist Lydekker recorded that otters were rare in Leicestershire, Rutland and Hertfordshire.

By 1950 there was growing concern among naturalists for the future of the otter, and in 1952 Marie Stephens conducted the first otter survey in this country, sponsored by the University Federation of Animal Welfare. Her report, published in 1957, did much to draw public attention to

British otter at the head of a weir.

the state of the otter in Britain. Although not unduly pessimistic at that time the years that followed quickly destroyed any tendency towards complacency. Pollution, both industrial and agricultural, increased on a large scale while the various Water Authorities built many more sewage works in rural areas to service villages and small towns, and they in turn poured vast quantities of effluent rich in phosphates and nitrogen into the country's waterways every day.

By 1955 a new form of pollution had arrived in the form of organo-chlorine insecticides, including dieldrin, aldrin and heptachlor used as agricultural seed dressings and in sheep dips. The sudden decline in Britain's bird of prey population, particularly peregrines and sparrow-hawks, following the use of these chemicals has been well documented, and scientists were able to show that dieldrin in particular was respon-sible for the deaths, not only of birds of prey, but of mammals as well, including foxes, badgers and otters. Two scientists in particular, Paul Chanin and Don Jefferies, demonstrated that the decline in otter num-bers from the late 1950s onwards reflected precisely the use of dieldrin.

Those areas of England from which the otter had virtually disappeared, the southern and eastern counties, were the arable areas using heavy applications of seed dressing, while in the north-west dieldrin was used in sheep dips. In both cases wild animals, including otters, accumulated significant and sometimes lethal levels of the chemical through the ingestion of prey species over a period of time.

Eventually the government responded to the alarm raised by conservationists and in 1975 the use of dieldrin for seed dressing and in sheep dips was banned. However, its use in industry was still allowed, and this resulted in the continued contamination of waterways, while both industry and agriculture continued to use polychlorinated biphenyls (PCBs) in increasing amounts, particularly in pesticides. PCBs are known to accumulate in freshwater fish and have been found in particularly high concentrations in herons. Otters too, living mainly on fish, have ingested lethal or sub-lethal doses. More recently unacceptable levels of heavy metals, particularly mercury and cadmium, have been found in the bodies of some otters.

The final factor causing the alarming decline of the otter was undoubtedly the destruction of habitat, resulting from the wide-scale draining of marshes, canalisation of rivers and the destruction of bankside trees and other vegetation carried out by the Water Authorities, coupled with the increase in disturbance caused by such activities as boating, canoeing, rambling, fishing and shooting.

At one time it was suggested that the American mink, having escaped from fur farms and established itself as a feral animal in many parts of England by the 1950s, could be helping to keep down otters, and there were rumours of mink having attacked and eaten young otter cubs. Since otters are four times bigger than mink and many times fiercer I always felt such claims to be unfounded, and since then scientists have shown that there is no truth in them. Studies in Sweden revealed that otters and mink cohabited successfully in the same areas, and furthermore that there was little competition for food as the otter, more adapted to aquatic life than the mink, lived mainly on fish, while mink, although preying on fish at times, relied more on small mammals, insects and frogs. Not only were there behavioural and feeding differences between mink and otter, but there were significant differences in the preferred habitat of the two species.

Between 1977 and 1979 a National Survey Programme (NSP) co-ordinated by Don Jefferies of the Nature Conservancy Council was carried out to determine the status of the otter in England, Wales and Scotland.

The result of this first National Survey fully justified conservationists' concern over the decline of the otter in England and Wales. In England only 6% of the 2,940 sites visited were positive, while in Wales, where the otter population had always been thought to be more secure, only 20% of the 1,030 sites surveyed showed signs of otters. In parts of north and south-east Wales and central England the otter had already disappeared, whilst in East Anglia and several other southern counties the otter populations were so sparse that it was doubtful if the animal would survive. In Scotland the situation was entirely different, with 73% of more than 4,000 sites visited proving positive.

Otter at the edge of a mill leet.

This then was the scenario when Jeanne and I founded the Otter Trust in 1971 as a registered public charity. The aims of the new Trust were fourfold: firstly, to promote the conservation of otters throughout the world wherever it was necessary for their survival; secondly, to maintain a collection of otters in semi-natural but controlled conditions, both for research and for the interest and education of the general public and of children in particular; thirdly, to carry out research into the breeding of otters in captivity, with the ultimate aim of releasing young animals wherever suitable habitat remained; and fourthly, to promote and support field studies of otters in order to collect factual scientific information to help in their management and conservation. Throughout almost the whole of western Europe otter populations had plummeted, and in many countries including Italy, France, Holland, Belgium and Germany, it was clearly threatened with extinction. In other parts of the world other species of otter were also threatened, but we felt that in those cases the Trust's main job would be to finance proper research and conservation methods to be carried out by scientists of the countries concerned. Jeanne and I knew only too well the kind of problems we would encounter in setting up a Trust of this kind, and in attempting to do anything worthwhile in the way of practical conservation. We knew that sooner rather than later the new Trust would have to stir public opinion to the point where the government would be forced to grant legal protection to the otter throughout Britain, and we also knew that otter hunters and many other field sports enthusiasts would violently oppose such an idea. In the battle which followed the Trust was able to put its weight behind arguments advanced by the Nature Conservancy Council, the County Naturalists' Trusts and other conservation organisations urging the otter's protection. Finally, despite tremendous opposition, the conservationists won, and on 1 January 1978 the otter was added to Schedule 1 of the list of animals protected in England and Wales under the 1975 Conservation of Wild Creatures and Wild Plants Act. More recently it has been accorded full protection throughout the British Isles under the Wildlife and Countryside Act 1981.

If the new Trust was to be effective it would need its own headquarters with sufficient land to enable us to carry out our ambitious breeding project, for this would entail at least twenty large semi-natural breeding enclosures. At the same time the whole area would have to be set up in such a way as to enable and encourage the public to see practical conservation in action – which would mean facilities including a tea room, shop, car park and an interpretative centre, as well as offices and of course the necessary staff to run the outfit. We searched for a suitable property for over two years and after a long battle failed to obtain planning permission for the first likely site to become available, near Hadleigh in Suffolk. One of our requirements was a good unpolluted water supply, preferably in the form of a small stream or river, and this greatly narrowed the choice of properties. We had begun to feel that nothing suitable would ever turn up when our land agent telephoned one morning to say that a small marsh farm in the Waveney valley on the border between Norfolk and Suffolk might be coming on to the market.

CHAPTER 5

River Farm

The low white farmhouse stood well back from the road and was approached by a short drive, down one side of which grew a tall and straggling hedge of hawthorn. Beyond it in a small paddock of rough grass with clumps of stinging nettles and a variety of old ironware pushed into the hedge to fill gaps, a black sow rooted contentedly round the base of an old crab-apple tree. On the other side a small lawn supported daffodils in regimental ranks and newly-planted apple trees evenly spaced in parallel lines. We knocked loudly on the front door with no result. Assuming nobody was at home, although the agent had told us that the owners who were selling the house were expecting us, we began to explore. Suddenly an upstairs window flew open revealing the tousled grey head of an elderly man who demanded to know what we wanted. We explained that we had come to view the house with the possibility of buying it, to which he replied that the owners were out and he did not know if it was for sale. With that the head disappeared and the window slammed shut.

Winter at Earsham, with River Farm in the background.

Jeanne and I retreated to the lane and drove a little way to take stock through a gap in the hedge. The house had a roof of old pantiles, the steepness of the pitch indicating that it had originally been thatched, and it was clearly Tudor in origin, although hardly improved by flimsy modern shutters bright with varnish and a red front door. Beyond the paddock there appeared to be a small range of serviceable farm buildings of old brick and flint in the traditional Norfolk style, and beside them an assortment of corrugated-iron buildings blotched red with rust. Beyond the house lay the marshes leading to the banks of the river Waveney.

I suppose most people enjoy looking at houses, particularly when they are not seriously considering a purchase, but in our case time was running out. Jeanne and I had sold our house at Great Witchingham near our Wildlife Park and were looking for a site upon which to set up the Otter Trust which we had founded some years previously. In the

Sam, our labrador, helped to rear two young otters whose mother had no milk.

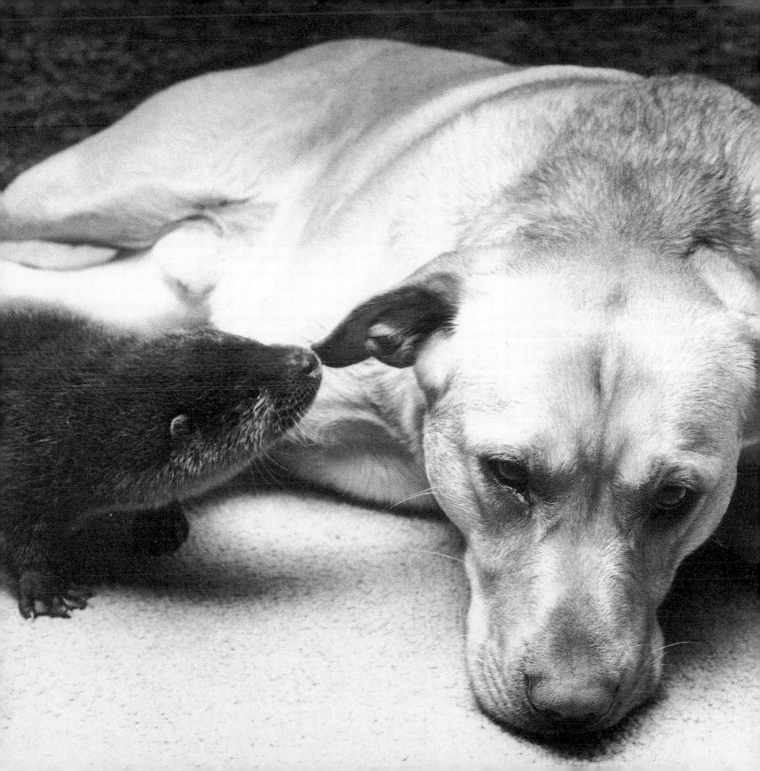

meantime the otters remained at our Norfolk Wildlife Park, though their accommodation, at least that of our hand-reared otters, left much to be desired. Kate and Lucy, the twin British otters, were living in a large dog kennel the concrete run of which was not to their liking, while Mouse, Jeanne's hand-reared Asian short-clawed otter, was housed in a small paddock surrounded by a wire netting fence with a wooden hut complete with an infra-red lamp in case the nights should turn cold.

Soon after that first visit we returned again to River Farm, and this time the owners welcomed us to tea and showed us the house. The agent had warned us that the ceilings were very low and the stairs steep, and he volunteered the information that the marshes flooded most winters. I agreed with him about the house, which I found dark and cramped and a little depressing, but Jeanne saw its potential and was quick to point out that there were signal advantages. The lane at the end of the drive used to be the main carriageway from Bungay to Harleston. Narrow and winding, it had been replaced a few years previously by a wide highway on the old railway track to the north, leaving the small road quiet and deserted. There were likely to be few problems of access when it came to gaining planning consent. Furthermore, the 14 acres of marshes bounded on the south by the river Waveney were ideal for our otter breeding enclosures. The land also included an attractive lake of 4 acres where gravel had been extracted some years previously. Two small spinneys and a line of ancient crack willows leaning over the placid waters of the Waveney completed the property, the general layout of which would enable us to keep the house and some 8 acres of land surrounding it separate from the Trust's headquarters and the breeding enclosures. Not least among its advantages was the distance from Great Witchingham, 30 miles, which would allow us to continue to run our Wildlife Park, where so many of the Trust's otters were born.

I have bought several properties in my life and have never found it particularly easy, not because I was unwilling to pay the purchase price, but simply because the vendor never really seemed to want to sell. Perhaps it's just my luck or perhaps nobody ever wants to part with an attractive place. River Farm was no exception. The vendors were

Digging the breeding pens.

charming and hospitable, and after several visits I even began to like the wattle and daub farmhouse with its oak beams – at least those which had not been covered with plasterboard. One week all seemed set and the vendor ready to exchange contracts. The next week we were back to square one because the vendor had changed his mind and thought he would rather not sell. This game of cat and mouse lasted all summer, but finally contracts were exchanged and on 1 October we took possession. Two days later an excavator on caterpillar tracks with a 22-foot boom lumbered down the ramp of a low-loader and crept like a prehistoric monster across the marsh, stopping at the side of the drainage channel which runs through the middle of our land. Untouched for decades, the stream had silted up and was little more than a shallow depression where sedge, reed and water celery flourished. We planned to construct the otter breeding enclosures in a long line with the stream running through all of them and to form a pool in each by digging out its banks. The excavator roared into life, opening the steel jaws of its bucket to rip up mouthfuls of dripping earth and vegetation which it dropped neatly on the marsh behind it. As it worked the peaty soil shook like jelly and brown liquid swirled in the ever widening channel for the water table was less than 2 feet below ground level.

By the end of the first day three pools were completed, but progress was soon to be slowed down by the soft ground in which the machine bogged down. It took three weeks to complete twenty-one pools, the black bank of dripping soil, higher than a man, growing longer each day. Our idea was to use the soil when it dried out to form a raised walkway right along the front of the enclosure so that visitors would not have the inconvenience of looking over a high fence to see the otters.

Within days Jeanne had enlisted the help of a local building firm whose men virtually took apart the old farmhouse. Like most wooden-framed houses in the valley ours was long and narrow, wide enough for a team of oxen to haul the massive frame of oak pillars and beams upright when wooden pegs driven into previously bored holes held the whole framework rigid. Clay and mud for the wattle and daub had been obtained by excavating a small pond nearby. Starting at one end in the living room the builders were instructed to remove a small tiled fireplace. Behind it lay barrow-loads of debris, but when it had been cleared out a Tudor hearth was revealed some 10 feet wide, complete with bread oven. Layers of lino were peeled from the floor to expose the original pamment tiles which, though badly worn, were as good as new when turned over and relaid. Above the living room two bedrooms were made into one by removing the partition wall. This involved raising a massive oak tie beam spanning the room 4 feet above the floor. We felt that some of our visitors might find the low door a little inconvenient, so we had two hefty steel brackets constructed, and when the builders had tied the house together by nailing a heavy baulk of timber across below the beam they cut through it and raised it 2 feet. During this operation the partition above the beam was taken down, revealing the original wattle and daub, basically stakes tied together with coarse string, then plastered with a mixture of mud and cow dung. The stakes had doubtless been cut from a nearby hedgerow. They were as sound as the day they were cut, and the coarse string was impossible to break with the bare hands, despite its four centuries of life.

Removal of a black iron grate in one of the bedrooms revealed a smaller Tudor hearth, and in the space between them the crumpled remains of *The News*, a weekly newspaper published at an early hour every Sunday evening at 'The News' office, number 28 Brydges-street, Covent-Garden, London. Number 647, published on 28 December 1817, although much torn, provides an illuminating miscellany of the sort of news items which interested the literate minority of those times. Apart from its interesting reflections on everyday life almost 170 years ago, the torn sheet gave us a fair idea of when the original Tudor fireplace was blocked up and replaced by the small black iron grate. Whether the newspaper was stuffed behind it intentionally or simply to get rid of it we shall never know. Along with it we found a tattered piece of an old ledger, some of the faded brown copperplate writing clearly legible. We read that on 14 December, the writer, whoever he was, was received from Mr Saunders 9 Clew 2 Skains.

Under Jeanne's supervision the interior of the house was considerably restored. Ceilings were stripped to reveal more oak beams, central heating was installed along with an additional bathroom and a new system of drains to a septic tank. By Christmas the house was ready for occupation.

During that period the maintenance staff and the manager came over daily from the Wildlife Park to work on the otter enclosures. All through the dark winter days they struggled in a sea of mud excavating trenches below the water table, driving in fencing stakes and putting up hundreds of metres of chain-link netting topped with an overhang of sheet steel. Gates were hung, thresholds concreted and electricity laid on to the fast growing line of enclosures.

Otters are efficient diggers, particularly if the ground is soft, and this meant that the fence to their large enclosures had to be sunk in the ground to a depth of about 3 feet. This necessitated using a small trenching machine, the principle of which was very simple. A single-

The breeding pens are as large and natural as possible.

cylinder petrol engine drove the main shaft which was attached to a chain carrying a number of equally-spaced small scoops. The engine also drove the winch on the front of the machine. The idea was to pull out the cable along the line the trench was to be dug, fasten the end securely to a tree or a post driven into the ground and then put the engine in gear. In theory, as the machine crept slowly forward, the winch drew in the cable, while at the same time the chain with its scoops gouged out a narrow trench to the required depth. In practice this was not as easy as it sounds. The tenacious peaty clay often refused to drop off the scoops so that the machine was constantly clogged. Roots and boulders caused it to veer from a straight course, while it seemed to find it easier to pull out the anchoring stake than to inch itself forward. Add to this a sea of mud like a World War I battlefield and you have a fair picture. But that was only the beginning, since once the posts and netting were in place the narrow trench had to be back-filled and this could only be done by hand. The sticky clay clung to the spades and formed huge balls round the men's feet making the work unbelievably backbreaking and frustrating.

The first otters were brought to River Farm a few days after we moved into the house. Naturally Kate and Lucy were the first to arrive, for we had made sure that their pens, which were nearest to the house, were also the first to be completed. Mouse, of course, had arrived with us and spent his days exploring the house, delving in the waste bin in the kitchen and generally making a nuisance of himself. He soon discovered how to open the door of the fridge and was found one afternoon happily chewing on a large fillet steak.

On the Saturday when I went back to Witchingham to collect Kate and Lucy, I felt a huge sense of relief as I returned with both of them safely in their boxes in the back of the car. Then Jeanne and I watched with pleasure as they enjoyed for the first time the expanse and depth of the pools in their new pens. Where the fence dividing the enclosures crossed the stream we had constructed stickles or barriers made of steel rods 2 inches apart in angle iron frames driven deep into the mud of the bottom of the stream. The top of each frame was clear of the water and fixed to the bottom of the pen. As the ends were embedded in each bank we felt sure that the stickles were otter-proof. How wrong we were.

Lucy, always more highly-strung than her sister Kate, had shown signs of stress during her time in the dog kennel, and before we had moved she had held Jeanne's leg tightly in her forepaws as if begging not to be left behind. For this reason we decided to release her into her new home first. When we opened the box she walked out quietly, turned to look at us and then slipped into the pool. For ten minutes or so she dived and spun, somersaulting and corkscrewing through the water in sheer joy. Then to our horror she disappeared and the water in her pool was still. My first thought was that she might have become wedged in the bars of the stickle, then Jeanne saw a movement in the stream outside the enclosure and there was Lucy happily playing. At first we were not unduly worried because she was accustomed to going for walks with us and swimming at liberty in the river or in the sea, and we rarely had any trouble in picking her up again when it was time to go home. Realising that she was in strange surroundings we both set off, mainly to keep in contact and give her confidence. Lucy thought the whole affair was great fun and kept running back to Jeanne only to dive off again whenever we attempted to catch her. Once she left the stream and crossed the raised bank along the river walk to dive into the main river. This caused us some concern since we could no longer keep up with her if she decided to go exploring. Twenty minutes later she returned and joined us as we walked back towards the house, but as we approached the pen she doubled back into the stream again. Once she came back to me and stood up, her forepaws resting against my legs, but when I bent down to pick her up she wriggled free, slippery as an eel. Dusk closed in and Lucy was beginning to show signs of tiring. She spent less time in the water, kept closer to us, and when Jeanne sat on the ground she climbed onto her lap. I assumed that the game was safely over but at that moment a low jet screamed over our heads and Lucy, terrified, fled back towards the river. We followed her in the gathering darkness and caught a glimpse of her as she ran down the bank into the main stream. She dived in at once and disappeared.

At first we waited, expecting her to show up, and when nothing happened we imagined she had gone off exploring again so we separated, Jeanne walking along the bank upstream calling to her while I did the same downstream. We kept it up for the next two hours but there was no sign of Lucy. Later that night I took a torch and walked up and down the river calling her name for more than an hour but saw nothing. At dawn I went out again walking the river and calling, but only the lapwings wailed in reply. We were both certain that Lucy would not have remained away unless she was lost, and during the following week we searched the river for miles upstream and down calling her name. We asked everyone locally to keep an eye open for her, and our staff spent hours joining in the search. With no news our hopes began to fade.

A month later the water level fell after an unusually dry spell. Along the river walk willow and alder boughs festooned with flotsam like old birds' nests were left high and dry by the receding floods. Patches of mud appeared at the river's edge and I searched for signs of otter tracks. Suddenly I noticed the top of a wooden stake, encrusted with weed and barely showing; the current eddying round it had caught my attention and from the stake a piece of rope trailed down into the murky depths. As I looked a cold shiver passed down my spine. Climbing down the bank I stretched out over the water using a broken-off bough to pull the rope towards me. It was covered by a layer of algae, grey-brown and slimy, and as I began to haul it in I knew the thing was evil. When I had enough slack I climbed up the bank and went on hauling at the dead weight. A line of corks appeared with dripping weed, then some netting and finally the bamboo hoop of an old eel trap broke the surface. The net was roughly 10 feet long, cylindrical in shape with two chambers, each with a funnel entrance. It was half full of mud and debris but there was something else in the first chamber – the body of a drowned otter. It was Lucy. We buried her that afternoon beneath the lawn, close to the house, and planted a lime tree over her grave. She must have entered the net out of curiosity and, being unable to find the way out again, had drowned, possibly while Jeanne stood on the bank above calling her. We both felt her loss, but it was much worse for Jeanne, as Lucy had always shown a special attachment for her and was very much her otter.

The fyke net in which Lucy met her death.

As soon as the house was finished the builders began the much bigger task of constructing the Trust's headquarters. Meanwhile the excavator had moved out onto the marshes to begin digging two lakes for waterfowl, each over 1¼ acres in size and 7 feet deep. Tens of thousands of loads of dripping peat were removed by a team of three dumpers and transferred to form a bank along the river's edge. When dry this would enable a bulldozer to reinforce the existing bank by piling the spoil 10 feet high along more than 500 yards of river, thus lessening the risk of flooding.

The lakes took three months to excavate, and two years passed before the soil dried out sufficiently for the bank to be graded. Since then it has been sown with grass seed, and today it is indistinguishable from the rest of the embankment which holds back the winter floods and protects the otter enclosures and our home from inundation should gale-force winds coincide with exceptionally high tides. Then the whole valley from Beccles to Diss, more than 20 miles, becomes a shimmering expanse studded with isolated thorn bushes and clumps of willows and alders knee-deep in the flood. Flocks of wintering Bewick swans and rafts of mallard and wigeon rest secure far from the shore, while in the partially flooded fields at the sides of the valley lapwings and golden plover spread out to feed at the water's edge.

From my dressing-room window I get an uninterrupted view across the marshes to the west where the dykes are studded with willows, and beyond them the trees, oak and alder, hiding the road into Suffolk; while to the south the uplands rise with a single farmhouse and its buildings etched on the skyline. To the east, above the willows, I can see the wooden spire of the village church with its golden weathervane gleaming in the sun. In winter black wedges of wildfowl flight up the valley against a dove-grey sky. Grey herons, quick to scavenge food left by the otters, have become absurdly tame and, when not sitting like grey sentinels still as posts on the marshes, fly lazily past with harsh cries. Sometimes in the early morning cormorants fly up the valley from the sea, black shapes wheeling on ragged wings before gliding down to join the waterfowl on the lake. If I open the window at night I hear the chuckle of passing mallard and the clear whistling whee-ohs of drake wigeon. In the lush green of high summer turtle doves call from the orchard while reed and sedge warblers rasp their songs from the thicket dividing our garden from the marsh. On the far side of the river black and white cattle graze and a lazy peace descends on the landscape.

By midsummer of that first year the months of effort began to show results. Twenty-one large breeding enclosures for otters with a raised walkway in front of them had been completed. The headquarters were well advanced, trees had been planted in the large car park and a fox-proof fence of heavy gauge galvanised weldmesh netting supported by pressure creosoted wooden posts, 8 feet high, had been erected round the perimeter of the entire property. Waterfowl from Great Witchingham swam on the three lakes and otters lived in thirteen of the twenty-one pens.

During that first summer Lucy's sister Kate gave birth to two fine cubs,

Eurasian otter and cubs in their holt.

a dog and a bitch whom we christened Lucy. Fittingly, they were the first British otter cubs to be born at Earsham and Jeanne and I felt a special thrill when we saw Kate bring them out for their first swim late one evening.

Gradually the new growth of grass and trees healed the scars made by the excavator, water plants of many species flourished in the otter pools and the marshes quickly reclaimed the raw edges of the new lakes. A concentrated final effort by everyone enabled us to open the Trust to visitors for the first time on 9 September, less than a year after we had taken possession of River Farm. However, for the next eighteen months work went on to complete the buildings and put the finishing touches to the Trust's grounds. Diminutive Muntjac deer were moved from Great Witchingham to live at liberty in the copse and reedbeds alongside the biggest lake. These little deer soon became remarkably tame and some will even take food from visitors' hands. On the Home Marsh in front of our house we established breeding flocks of western bean geese and lesser white-fronted geese, both species nesting in the wild in Lapland where their numbers had declined drastically in recent years owing to disturbance on their northern breeding grounds, which are invaded by increasing numbers of tourists every summer. The Swedish conservation authorities had just started a scheme for reintroducing captive-bred geese of these two species to the wild using feral Canada geese as foster-parents, and young birds of both species bred at Earsham were soon to play their part in this project. Chinese water-deer and demoiselle cranes were moved to a large paddock near our house, and along the river walk work began on an aviary enclosing mature willows where we hoped to establish a breeding colony of night herons.

That first summer finally faded into autumn, and I remember our amazement when we woke up one winter's morning and looked out of the bedroom window to see that the marshes, which were green the day before, had disappeared during the night beneath an inland sea which covered the whole of the Waveney valley. A carpet of silver-grey water stretched upstream and downstream as far as we could see, the surface broken only by the stark black branches of isolated thorn bushes and willow trees, while the tops of barbed-wire fences showed the position of the boundary dykes with here and there an old gatepost breaking the surface. Rafts of wildfowl and gulls roosted peacefully far from either shore. Our own marshes were inundated and the water had crept to within 30 yards of the house. We were surprised at the swiftness of the transition, and found it difficult to believe our builders who had told us when they were renovating the house that they were quite sure it had never been flooded because there were no watermarks inside the walls. Nevertheless, we anxiously phoned Anglian Water to ask how much further they expected the level to rise. They were reassuring, and at the same time offered to send out two men with a van laden with sandbags which they very kindly helped us to fill to block a low place in the river bank. I remember pushing a stake into the water and marking the level with a notch on one side. Every hour or so during the day I went out to look at it and each time the water had risen just a little bit higher. The locals assured us that should we be unlucky enough to have heavy rain within the next twenty-four hours the house would undoubtedly be flooded, but fortunately that did not happen, and by the following morning the level was once again below my notch.

The house has never been flooded since we have lived in it, although on several occasions the river has risen even higher than it did that first time. Nor are we necessarily immune during the summer months, for a period of torrential rain following a dry spell when the ground is hard will often result in flash floods caused by surface water rushing off the high ground on each side of the valley too fast for the river to contain it. These floods are nearly always short-lived, but quite impressive while they last. Sometimes the river disappears altogether and becomes a mere trickle between high banks of dripping black mud. Normally the sluice-gates further down the valley hold up the level of the river and are only opened by increased water pressure at the time of floods. But on occasion a fallen tree or large branch carried downstream will become lodged under one or more of the sluice-gates, and the river escapes overnight into Oulton Broad and the sea.

Lucy's tragic death meant that the stickles dividing the enclosures where they crossed the stream had to be redesigned. At first we tried driving wooden stakes deep into the mud with an inch gap between them. However even this proved ineffective since, while it was possible to gauge the distance at the top, there was no means of knowing what was happening 4 feet down beneath the surface of the muddy water. The otters invariably found any place where the stakes had spread slightly and it was surprising what a narrow gap they could squeeze through. We lost no more otters this way, but they were constantly getting into each other's pens with the risk of fighting, and I spent many winter mornings

British otter with twelve-week-old cubs at the Otter Trust.

clad in a wetsuit crawling along the bottom of the pools in thick mud feeling for any gaps in the stickles. I remember finding such a gap on a particularly cold morning when we had to break the ice before I could get into the water. Two posts had spread some 4 inches apart right at the bottom, and we decided to drive in a third stake to cover the hole. Crouching in the water I held the stake in position while Ronnie, one of our maintenance men, wielded a 14-pound sledgehammer to knock it in. Suddenly there was a rush of air past my left ear as the head of the sledgehammer flew off, missing my head by inches, and leaving Ronnie holding the weightless shaft.

In those early days many of our members became involved with the Trust's work, and I shall always remember the family who arrived a few days after we had opened and seemed bent on doing something practical in the form of outside work. It is much more difficult than it may sound to find jobs for people who turn up on the spur of the moment with little or no specialised knowledge, but on that occasion we had just finished reseeding the land round one of the lakes which came to be called the Trout Lake, and in doing so had uncovered a tremendous number of large flints where a house had stood more than a hundred years earlier. Jeanne had the bright idea of asking them to clear away all the stones, which they did most efficiently. They seemed to enjoy it, although I am sure they might have thought twice about volunteering had they known that it would involve a few hours' backbreaking stone picking!

So many members of the public seemed to want to become more involved with the Trust that in the end we set up an otter adoption scheme whereby anyone could adopt a given otter and pay for its food for a year. They could also choose the animal's name. I don't know why, but I have never really been in favour of such a scheme, perhaps because it seems too commercial. In our case the number of otters available for adoption was so small that I felt it was hardly worthwhile, and in the end we gave it up because we found it so difficult to write to people when their particular otter died, and found it even harder to write begging letters every year to those who had not paid their dues under the adoption scheme.

Kate and her four-month-old cub.

CHAPTER 6

Mouse

While we were primarily concerned with studying and breeding the British otter at the Trust, we had at that time two other species in the collection, the Indian smooth-coated otter which, as its name suggests, comes from Asia and is somewhat larger than its European cousin, and several pairs of Asian short-clawed otters. We felt that showing these two additional species would provide added interest for our visitors and would enable them to compare different types of otter, for while the British otter is solitary, shy and nocturnal, both the Asian species are social, diurnal and vociferous. In both these species the pair bond is strong and the male helps to bring up the cubs, which means that the pair can remain together throughout their lives. Playful and inquisitive, they are active throughout the day, which means that visitors always have something interesting to watch.

Asian short-clawed otters are the smallest of the world's nineteen species. They inhabit low-lying swamps, small streams and paddy fields in India, Indo-China and Malaysia. Their pair bonds are so strong that a couple nearly always move together as a single unit, chittering and squeaking to keep in contact. Just as shy and secretive in the wild as the European species, short-clawed otters are sometimes seen in daylight, although being crepuscular they are most active when daylight begins to fade. Jeanne and I have spent many mosquito-ridden nights in Malaysia crouched at the edge of a paddy field listening to a family party of these otters hunting frogs, fish and other small creatures, the constant twittering of the members of the group keeping us aware of their movements.

Hand-rearing otters is never easy, but I do not know of anyone apart from Jeanne who has attempted to rear an otter from the day it was born. As I described in an earlier book, *The River People* (1976), she had to

Jeanne bottle-feeding Mouse when he was less than a week old, watched by his parents Freckie and Kuala.

A pair of Asian short-clawed otters with their litter of five cubs.

do this in the case of Mouse because his mother had no milk and the rest of the litter had already died. It was a remarkable achievement, and resulted in the tamest otter of all time and one who was completely devoted to Jeanne and imprinted on her. Having never seen or experienced another otter, he was quite convinced that Jeanne was his natural mother – a classic situation for complete imprinting, when a young animal accepts a foster parent as his real parent. When she first held him in the palm of her hand he was no bigger than a mouse, which was how he got his name.

He thoroughly approved of our move to River Farm as the house was

Mouse debating whether to wake Jeanne.

much larger than our cottage at Great Witchingham, giving him far more scope for adventure and exploration. Furthermore, we had made our garden otter-proof so we had no fear of his wandering off and getting lost if somebody left a door open. At night we put him in a playpen 6½ feet square made of small-mesh wire netting on a wooden frame. This we put in the utility room with an infra-red lamp hanging over it for warmth. A cardboard box in one corner with bedding in it, a water bowl and a tray of sand to act as a latrine satisfied all his requirements. We found that Mouse was much easier to housetrain than a British otter, and he would run from one end of the house to the other to get back to his spraint tray rather than make a mess anywhere else.

His day began with the morning tea, which I usually make. When it was ready I would pick up the tray and lifting Mouse from his playpen put him under one arm and carry him up to our bedroom. As soon as he saw Jeanne he would start twittering and struggling until I dropped him on the bed, when he would run up on to the pillow, duck beneath the bedclothes and run to the foot of the bed where he invariably settled down to snooze clasping one of Jeanne's ankles firmly in both front paws. If she moved he twittered in annoyance and even when she got up he

Mouse asleep in bed.

Mouse was a master juggler.

usually remained asleep in the bed. There was no harm in this unless we forgot him, and then after an hour or two nature would call and he tended to come up from the depths of the bed to spraint on Jeanne's pillow!

Like all otters he was intensely curious and mischievous, poking and prying into every corner and doing his best to open cupboards, drawers and the fridge, not to mention the garbage bucket in the kitchen, which he regarded as a real treasure house, soon learning to operate the hinged lid. His intelligence was astonishing and we were constantly attempting new ways of thwarting some of his more destructive pranks. In time our house began to look a little odd with a playpen and its infra-red lamp in the utility room, the fridge tied up with string, a massive weight placed on top of the garbage bin and the three drawers in the unit to one side of the sink beneath the draining board devoid of handles. Mouse was in the habit of using the three handles, which were in a line vertically, as the rungs of a ladder to climb up onto the drainage board and thence into the sink. This was all very well but was inclined to be messy and distinctly heavy on crockery as glasses, dishes and plates were pushed over the edge to shatter on the floor beneath.

One evening he had been particularly destructive, and I decided the time had come to stop this escapade, so, grabbing a screwdriver, I took off all three drawer handles in an attempt to thwart him. This was all very well except that we had to prise open the drawers with a knife which was inconvenient, but at least it stopped Mouse climbing up. But not for

Mouse investigates the contents of Jeanne's bag.

long. One day Jeanne watched Mouse busily fiddling at the edge of the bottom drawer. She discovered to her amazement that he had brought a tiny stone in from the garden and was busy wedging it between the front of the drawer and the side of the unit. Short-clawed otters tend to bung up all holes with anything they can find – sticks, pebbles, grass, any objects small enough for them to carry by clamping them to their side with one forepaw while running on the other three legs. We do not claim that Mouse was consciously using the stone as an implement to prise open the drawer, but his efforts resulted in the drawer moving just enough for him to get his nimble rubbery little front paws into the crack along the top and pull it open. In no time at all he was in the open drawer and fiddling frantically at the bottom of the one above. Sure enough, he had soon opened it sufficiently to get his paws inside and pull it the rest of the way out. Climbing into that drawer he repeated the process with the one above and was soon back up on the draining board. New measures were called for and we hit on the idea of strong magnets which would clamp the drawers firmly shut and which we felt sure would prove too much for him. The only trouble was that we could not prise the drawers open ourselves, so we had to go out and buy some round brass knobs. Even with these the drawers had to have a sharp jerk to open them. This really did defeat him, and although we feared that he might find a way of climbing the knobs to gain access to the draining board he never did.

Mouse loved company and was particularly fond of our old gardener Jim, who, slow and unhurried in his movements, made the perfect companion as far as Mouse was concerned, especially as he was always doing something interesting. When he was digging there were worms to be pulled out of the ground and played with. When he was planting seeds there were the packets to be stolen and explored, and if Jim was planting peas Mouse was in his element for these were just the size for him to extract from the packets and spread about. Sometimes he lay on his back with his front paws in the air dexterously juggling three peas above his chest. The greenhouse was a source of particular joy, especially when it came to watering tomatoes. Then Mouse would run chittering after Jim holding out his paws to let the water cascade over them. Jim kept up a

Mouse helps in the greenhouse.

low muttered conversation nearly all the time and in reply Mouse chittered happily.

I remember once watching Jim planting onions in a neat and orderly row with Mouse following along behind and occasionally uprooting one as if to make sure that the job was being done to his satisfaction.

During our first summer Jeanne used to put Mouse out during the morning on the Home Marsh in front of the house so that he could explore the whole 7½ acres at his leisure. We were not afraid of losing him because the area was surrounded by a fox-proof fence to protect the waterfowl, while between our garden and the edge of the marsh was a low netting fence to prevent the geese from wandering in and eating all the plants. At first Mouse was rather daunted by the sheer space, and if otters can suffer from agoraphobia I think he probably did because for some days he kept very close to the garden fence and was usually at the gate waiting when Jeanne went to bring him in. Gradually however he gained confidence and roamed far and wide. Then one day disaster struck. Jeanne went out as usual to collect Mouse just before lunch but there was no sign of him. At first she was not worried and began to walk round the marsh and along the edge of the lake calling, but there was no reply. After half an hour and a thorough search she returned to the house and told me that Mouse had disappeared. We set off again together and searched both marshes without success. By now we were getting worried and all the staff joined in. Between us we walked the riverbank up and downstream and searched every nook and cranny of the buildings and the rest of the grounds, all to no avail. By mid-afternoon Jeanne and I were wondering what to do when suddenly a car stopped at the end of our drive and a young girl came towards us.

'My father and I have just seen an otter. Have you lost one?' she asked in a most casual manner. This sounded too good to be true and, trying to keep the excitement out of my voice, I replied:

'Yes, we have, but tell me, how big was the otter you saw?'

'Oh, quite small, not much over a foot long and it was playing in a puddle at the side of the Flixton road at the entrance to the gravel pits.'

'How long ago was this?'

'Less than twenty minutes, because we've driven straight here.'

Thanking her for her trouble, Jeanne and I jumped into the car and shot off down the valley towards Homersfield where the road crosses the river and back on the far side towards Flixton. We were both silent during the drive, and for the same reason. The Flixton road was straight and busy, cars and lorries hurtling along at speed, and it would be a deathtrap for a small otter. The entrance to the gravel pits was in constant use by heavily-laden lorries, and we could picture Mouse squashed flat beneath their enormous wheels. When we reached the gravel pits there was no sign of Mouse, but at least we had not found him run over. The puddles were there all right, but we had no means of telling which way Mouse had gone. Walking into the gravel works we went up to the office where the foreman confirmed that he had seen a small otter playing in the entrance only about half an hour before. In fact while he watched it it had crossed the main Flixton road and disappeared into a belt of trees on the other side. He volunteered to show us exactly where Mouse had gone and led us over the road, down a track through the trees which ended in a gate on to the marshes. Thanking him, we separated, Jeanne walking along the edge of the trees to the west while I followed a similar route to the east. Both of us constantly called Mouse by name and it was our intention to walk a mile or more before traversing the marsh to join the riverbank and return along it. I was on my way back and was within shouting distance of Jeanne who appeared to be coming towards me. Suddenly I realised she was no longer calling Mouse but *my* name. Fearing the worst I ran towards her.

'What's happened?' I shouted.

'I've heard him,' she replied, 'but I can't see him.'

'Are you sure it was him?'

'Yes, of course I am,' she replied as she led me towards the belt of trees by the road. 'This is where I first heard him, and then I saw him under those trees, but as there's no way across the dyke I've had to stay here to keep an eye on him until you came.'

She had hardly finished speaking when we heard Mouse's unmistakable welcoming squeaks, and then we saw him paddling about in the

Jeanne takes Mouse for a walk on the flooded marshes.

leaves beyond the dyke. Leaving me to watch him Jeanne set off to cross over where the track joined the marsh. Soon I heard her coming, and so did Mouse. Squeaking with delight he ran towards her and straight into her arms. Our relief knew no bounds as we carried him back to the car.

We shall never know why he went so far or what route he took, but most surprising of all was the fact that he must have crossed the river Waveney. We could hardly believe this because, brought up in our house, Mouse was rather afraid of water, and while he was happy in a small pool or puddle we could never persuade him to swim in anything larger. What possessed him to cross the expansive river, which is nearly 20 yards wide, we shall never know. We can only assume that in exploring a steep part of the bank he may have fallen in and, finding it impossible to climb back up the slope, had swum across to the low-lying marshes opposite where he could land easily. I am sure he was intelligent enough to do that, and having landed he presumably wandered off in the hope of eventually reaching home.

Every day during the summer Jeanne would take Mouse for a walk in the Trust's grounds so that as many visitors as possible would be able to meet him. He was always a tremendous attraction and when safely in Jeanne's arms would allow strangers to stroke him. At other times he would follow her unerringly through a forest of human legs twittering his contact call but never for a moment losing track of her. I especially remember one afternoon when a blind girl was brought to the Trust. Jeanne introduced her to Mouse and she was able to hold him and by stroking him and holding his paws she felt she really knew him. Later on we took her to meet my tame European eagle owl, Bubo, who at that time had been with us for more than twenty years. Bubo was extraordinarily tame and once again she was able to stroke her and feel the bird's size and shape, riffling her fingers through Bubo's soft feathers. She remarked that it had been one of the most exciting afternoons of her life.

In those early days our secretary spent every Friday counting up the week's takings, working out the PAYE and putting up the staff's wages. Sitting at a table surrounded by notes, coins and tillrolls she checked the amounts, sorted the cash and put it into various bags.

This was Mouse's favourite day, and he would climb up into her lap and from thence on to the table and join in the sorting. Squealing with delight he would plunge his forepaws into any bank bag he could find, riffling through the coins inside. The smallest coins, particularly half-pence, delighted him most. These he would carry away to cache in any convenient crevice in the chair or table.

People often asked why Mouse did not appear on television, and the reason was that I felt it unfair to drag him round the country from one studio to another. Jeanne took him on a BBC Schools programme once, and while it was a success and they both came over well Mouse did not enjoy it. The local premiere of *Tarka the Otter*, produced and directed by our friend David Cobham, at the Noverre Cinema in Norwich was another matter. As Jeanne had hand-reared the star of the film, Tarka, and much of it had been filmed either at our Wildlife Park or at the Trust

Mouse in contemplative mood.

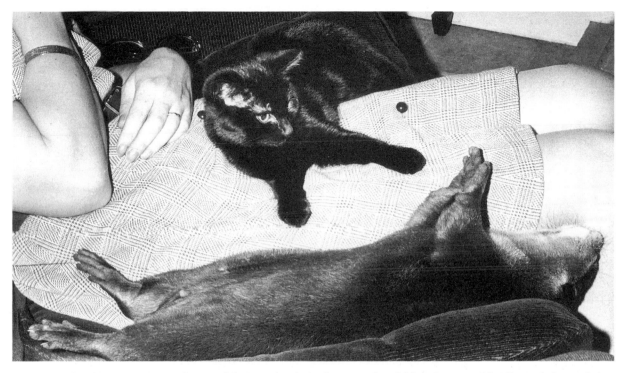

Mouse and Milly the cat.

it was felt appropriate that we should be there on the first night and that Mouse should accompany us. He enjoyed the short journey into Norwich sitting on Jeanne's lap, and I suppose the foyer, thronged with people, was for him little different from an afternoon crowd at the Trust. Feeling totally secure in Jeanne's arms he welcomed the audience, allowing countless strangers to stroke him while he chittered contentedly.

Always afraid of deep water, Mouse was in his element when the winter floods covered the marsh, for then the water nearest the house was not more than an inch or two deep, and during his daily walk he would follow Jeanne through the shallows paddling about in ecstasy, his forepaws forever active below the surface feeling for any small object which might be edible or even useful as a plaything. I was always fascinated by the dexterity of his tactile paws, so like little rubbery human fingers. When searching beneath the surface of the water he would move his paws from side to side, the 'fingers' moving as if playing a piano, instantly receptive to the feel of anything alive or dead. During this process Mouse wore an abstract expression, never looking at where his paws were feeling but gazing around him in a most unconcerned way.

It was during our first summer at River Farm that we acquired a companion for Mouse in the form of a cat. We happened to be over at Great Witchingham one day when our barn cat was playing amongst the sacks in the barn with her latest litter of kittens. We had always kept barn cats to keep down the mice and rats, and through a process of selection we had produced a jet-black race. I think they may have had Siamese blood in them at some time because apart from being rather slim and long in the leg they were also talkative and had large owl-like eyes. Jeanne could not resist one of the tiny black kittens and, picking it up, took it back to River Farm where we installed it in a cardboard box in the kitchen. It was christened Milly and it grew up in the house and soon became tame and confiding with us, though always remaining somewhat aloof in the presence of strangers. In the fullness of time it became clear that Milly was about to become a mother, and there was much discussion as to where she would have the kittens. I felt the best place was in a cardboard box in our hall, a warm room where they could do little harm on the pamment floor and where there were a number of secluded and rather gloomy corners. Taking a box I cut an entrance hole in one end and put it in the quietest and darkest place. Carrying Milly from the kitchen I pushed her through the entrance into the box, saying to her, 'That's where you will have to have your kittens.' Having been put in a cardboard box when first brought to River Farm she seemed to approve of the idea, and in the days to come we often noticed her sleeping inside the box. Sure enough that was exactly where she did have her kittens, five of them, three of which were jet black. We found homes for four but kept the remaining kitten, a little black female whom Jeanne christened Petal.

Milly had always treated Mouse with respect, keeping her distance, and for his part he tended to ignore her although sometimes both of them would curl up and sleep happily in the same armchair. In Petal's case it was different because she had never known life without Mouse and so accepted him from the start.

Curious by nature, Mouse always enjoyed new places and experiences and I well remember taking him on a day's outing to the Norfolk Broads. At the time we were making a film for the 'Survival' series on Independent Television and we needed a shot of an otter on a riverbank looking at a passing Broads cruiser. This was not an easy thing to accomplish, but a friend who ran a boatyard volunteered to help, so one sunny morning five of us set off in a motorboat from the yard to cruise downriver towards Breydon Water in search of a suitable place. Having found a spot where the bank was reasonably elevated and level, with a fringe of reeds at the water's edge, we landed and Jeanne took Mouse ashore. He was soon busy exploring the creeks and gullies feeling with feverish activity in all the crevices and beneath the overhanging marsh plants.

Meanwhile I set up the camera and recording equipment in a position where the river would form the background and Mouse on the bank would, I hoped, be in the foreground. That was fine, but the problem remained how to induce Mouse to remain roughly in the right area and to take any interest at all in the passing boat, while at the same time of course Jeanne had to remain out of shot. To complicate things clouds were now moving slowly but surely across the sky and it was essential that this particular shot should be taken in sunlight in order to match in with the rest of the sequence. Getting a boat to pass at the moment when the sun was out and Mouse was on the spot and looking suitably surprised on cue took quite a long time, but in the end we achieved it. The sun shone brightly, and just as a large cruiser was approaching Jeanne managed to persuade Mouse to follow her to the edge of the bank. As the boat approached she slipped out of shot behind him and deftly threw a clod of earth into the water a few feet away. This attracted Mouse's attention, but as he moved towards the spot the boat roared past. Mouse stopped dead in his tracks, then, moving a few paces backwards, stood up on his hind legs and stared in astonishment at the huge and noisy craft.

As long as he was with Jeanne, Mouse showed very little fear of things much larger than he was. Perhaps this was because during his early days we had in our garden a hand-reared roe deer called Chloe. She had been orphaned as a small kid when her mother was hit by a car on one of the main roads through Thetford Chase. Brought to us, Jeanne had reared her by hand. Of course she became absurdly tame and we didn't have the heart to put her with our herd of roe deer which had the run of a wood and a small meadow in the Park. Instead Chloe lived in the garden and often ventured through the back door and into the kitchen. Wary and shy of strangers, and especially of dogs, she was completely confident with us, and she and Mouse became good friends, playing together on the lawn. The form of play was amusing to watch because Mouse would rush up to Chloe and playfully nip her just above one of her hind hooves. Chloe would immediately dance away sideways only to wait for Mouse to make a renewed attack, when she would spin round and, lowering her head, pretend to butt him, when really she was only blowing at him. They sometimes kept up this game for minutes on end.

Although otters can live for fifteen years or even more this is an exception, and as with dogs ten to twelve years is a longish life for an otter. Mouse was not to be so lucky. In those early days we had lost two or three otters from kidney stones, small deposits consisting of calcium and salts which build up in the kidneys, eventually causing renal failure. We were at a loss to understand the cause of this as we had always taken particular care with our otters' diet. However, as soon as we realised the threat of kidney failure we immediately did everything we could to reduce the amount of calcium in their food. Perhaps we did not do this quite soon enough to save Mouse, for in the autumn of his fifth year he began to lose weight and became generally listless, taking little interest in his food. The X-rays showed nothing, the antibiotics made no difference. For a week Mouse was hand-fed and lived in the utility room under an infra-red lamp, but each day found him more lethargic. He died quietly one morning from what was later diagnosed as kidney failure. Jeanne's feeling of loss can be imagined, for Mouse was unique. Nobody had reared an otter from such a tiny beginning, and probably no otter had done more for conservation than Mouse. He personified the Otter Trust in the minds of the hundreds of thousands of visitors who had met him during his regular daily walks round the Trust's grounds over the years, and it is probably true to say that through his close contact with such a large number of people Mouse contributed more to the conservation of otters by arousing public interest and concern than any human being has done. For five years he gave affection to Jeanne and me and our family as well as endless pleasure to all those who met him. Handicapped children and adults, particularly the blind and those in wheelchairs, were able to cuddle Mouse and through him to know what an otter was really like.

Mouse in a friendly mood. Note the absence of claws on the highly sensitive front paws.

CHAPTER 7

Preparing the Ground

When the Trust first opened some of our visitors were surprised at the youthfulness of our staff, but this was because Jeanne and I had always felt that wherever possible young people should be employed in conservation, if only for their idealism and unbounded enthusiasm. Of course for some the tedium of daily routine soon tarnishes both, but not for all.

Our first 'manager' turned up on our doorstep one night and announced that rather than stay on at school and take his A levels he had decided, much against his father's wishes, to leave at the end of the current term and would like a job at the Otter Trust. We were so impressed by his obvious keenness and determination that we gave him one on the spot. The fact that he came from a farming family and that his father's land adjoined ours were factors in his favour, but he soon proved himself and within a few months we made him Trainee Manager with two other equally young members of staff to work with him. They were principally concerned with the daily feeding of the otters, waterfowl and deer and the unending grasscutting both in the otter enclosures and elsewhere.

One of the problems of a marsh farm is that owing to the dampness of the soil the grass is always growing. This is fine for graziers, but not so good when pens, paths and lawns have to be kept neat and tidy for visitors, which entails weekly cutting. For large areas like the marshes themselves we use a tractor with a mounted and power-operated cutter 6 feet wide, while for the otter pens and smaller areas we have always used small petrol-driven cutters which have to be pushed manually. In hot weather this is hard work, and it has to be done day after day. In the winter there are other maintenance jobs to be done, and we soon found

An enclosure for Asian short-clawed otters at Earsham.

out some of the problems associated with building otter enclosures on soil which overlies shifting peat. When we first excavated the pools they were all 6 feet deep in the centre, but within a few months we noticed that the water was appreciably shallower, and then we realised that it was rather like digging a hole on a sandy beach at low tide when the sides keep creeping inwards to fill up the bottom. Nor was this the only problem, since the otters, although not compulsive burrowers like badgers, soon discovered the joys of working away at the waterlogged soil at each end of the stickles or barriers dividing their enclosures across the communal stream. Always quick to take advantage of anything in their favour, they did most of their burrowing at water level where the earth was softest and where the water itself helped their excavations. To counter this we drove in more steel plates as piling in every enclosure, and as these were rather unsightly we covered them by building rockwork of natural carr stone against them.

The design and layout of the Trust buildings in those early days was done by Jeanne, who not only acted as general supervisor, but was responsible for everything from organising staff to public relations and

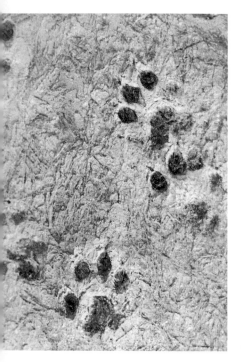

British otter footprints in the mud.

dealing with members while at the same time overseeing the renovation of our farmhouse. One day a slender girl in her early twenties, her long hair streaming in the wind, arrived in search of a job. Jeanne interviewed her and decided she might be quite good, and to test her reactions as much as anything she said, 'If you want to work for us at this stage you'll have to do everything from scrubbing the tea-room floor and serving in the shop to otter conservation as well as being Membership Secretary.' Lizzie was an Oxford Arts graduate but had always taken a keen interest in conservation, and soon picked up the basic principles of the Trust's work. She combined a warm and pleasant personality with a quick brain and a flair for design.

To Lizzie fell the brunt of the first really major fieldwork ever carried out by the Trust. Our basic aims were twofold: firstly, to build up a large breeding stock of European otters in captivity in order to have a surplus of cubs for reintroduction to the wild every year wherever we could find suitable habitat still remaining; secondly, to create otter havens or sanctuaries along all the rivers in East Anglia where otters still occurred or had been present in the not-too-distant past. With few exceptions it is almost impossible to conserve otters on the lower stretches of rivers where the waterway is navigable and subject to disturbance from human activities ranging from sailing, canoeing, motorboating, waterskiing and angling to just walking along its banks. In most cases the lower navigable reaches of rivers are publicly owned and controlled by the Port and Haven Commissioners or other official bodies. Thus it follows that the future of the otter lies largely in the upper and narrower reaches of lowland rivers, which are generally privately owned. In such cases there is usually little or no public access, no boating, and the fishing is privately controlled. We soon realised that it was to the landowners that we must look for the survival of the otter over large areas of Britain.

The practice of establishing otter havens on rivers started in Holland, where the results were said to have been encouraging. The idea is that particularly favourable stretches should be declared strict or maximum security havens (M areas), in which ideally there would be no boating or angling, no public access and where bankside vegetation would be

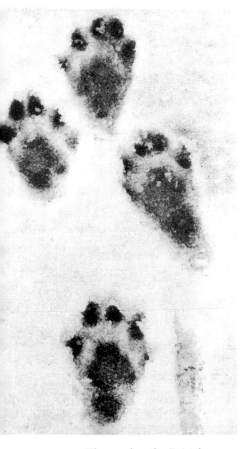

The tracks of a British otter in the snow. You can tell that the animal is walking because the tracks of the hind paws have been left behind those of the front. When it moves fast, the back feet pass over the front feet, leaving prints in front.

allowed to flourish and weedcutting and other management practices reduced to a minimum. Such maximum security areas would ideally be linked by less strictly controlled reaches of the river where otters would still be protected but where there might be limited angling and boating with public access confined to one bank. These would be known as protection or P areas. It was obvious that such havens could only be set up with the full co-operation of the landowners concerned as well as that of the local Water Authority and in many cases the anglers. It was clearly going to be a mammoth task, and one which anyone less enthusiastic and determined than Lizzie would have found daunting.

If we were to succeed we had to know who owned all the land along all the rivers throughout the whole of East Anglia. We imagined that this would not prove too difficult, since we assumed that the Water Authority maintained records of all riparian owners. How wrong we were! I telephoned the official concerned at Anglian Water to explain why we wanted the names and addresses of all riparian owners only to be told that they had no such list.

'Surely,' I said, 'you must have, because when you want to carry out maintenance works on any particular stretch of privately-owned river I always understood that you informed the landowner first.'

'Oh yes, of course we always do,' he replied, 'but we leave that to the local foreman, the man on the ground. He usually lives in the village and therefore knows who owns all the various farms along the river, and we leave it to him to contact the farmers and landowners concerned before we enter their land, but I can assure you we keep no records of owners or their properties either here at our headquarters or anywhere else.'

This was a setback which would have to be overcome. Fortunately I had lived in Norfolk for more than thirty-five years and so I knew a great many of the landowners and was able to provide Lizzie with a list of several names and addresses on all the rivers of Norfolk. Starting with these she telephoned each one and made an appointment to see them so that she was able not only to explain our otter haven project and seek their support for it, but also to find out the names and addresses of adjoining landowners. By repeating the process she was eventually in a

Typical track of a British otter in the snow.

position to compile a complete register of all the riparian owners on the river systems of the county. This entailed hundreds of miles of travelling, but once completed we were able to enter the next phase. For this we made up a package for every landowner containing an illustrated leaflet explaining the otter's decline and its possible causes and how they could help by co-operating with our otter haven scheme. In addition we included a letter introducing Lizzie and explaining exactly what she was doing together with a very short questionnaire containing five boxes which were to be ticked or not as the case might be. The purpose of this was to make sure that each landowner had given permission for Lizzie to enter their land, and for her to know from the form whether she had to make contact first before every visit or not. Having always experienced some difficulty in filling in forms myself I made sure that the five questions were brief and unambiguous and required no writing. Finally, we also sent each landowner a letter to the Master of the local Otter Hounds asking him not to hunt mink or coypu on his land since the disturbance caused would be just as damaging as hunting the otters themselves, which was of course illegal. All the landowner had to do was sign the letter and send it off in a stamped addressed envelope which we provided.

The response exceeded all our expectations, and only three land-owners refused to co-operate in any way. Next Lizzie opened a file for each of the eleven river systems in Norfolk. The file contained the names, addresses and telephone numbers of all the landowners on that river together with a code number. Large-scale maps of the river were drawn and divided into sections upon each of which the relevant land-owner's code number was marked showing the extent of his particular haven and whether it was an M or a P area. For every haven a registration form was completed giving the name of the river, the code number of the riparian owner, the grid reference number at the centre of the haven, the nearest village, the date of the agreement with the owner, the name of the Water Authority, the type of haven, the total length of haven, the approximate depth of water, the width of the river, the flow, the fish species, the bankside vegetation, the macrophytes or water plants and whether or not mink were thought to be there, whether otters were present and any proposals for changes to the habitat such as planting more cover. Finally the dates on which the relevant organisations including the Water Authority, the Nature Conservancy Council and the county Naturalists' Trust were notified of the haven were included together with a brief description of the haven and any pertinent remarks. These forms were to provide invaluable information on Norfolk rivers and would enable us to compile an ecological summary of all of them – something which had never been attempted before.

The second entrance to a holt in a bank.

Looking for signs of otters along the banks of the River Wissey.

─────── *The Number of Sites on Norfolk Rivers with* ───────
Evidence of Otters 1980–81

River	No. of sites visited	No. of sites with otters S	No. of sites with otters W	Total no. of sites with otters	Additional records
ANT	17	0	0	0	0
BABINGLEY	6	0	1	1	0
BAS	7	1	0	1	0
BLACKWATER	6	0	0	0	0
BURE	39	0	0	0	2
BURN	8	0	0	0	0
CHET	8	0	0	0	0
CUT-OFF CHANNEL	11	1	1	1	0
GAYWOOD	1	0	0	0	0
GLAVEN	17	4	6	6	3
GREAT OUSE	8	0	0	0	0
HEACHAM	30	0	0	0	0
INGOL	3	0	0	0	0
LITTLE OUSE	10	0	0	0	0
MERMAID	2	0	0	0	0
MUCK FLEET	4	1	1	1	0
NAR	22	0	0	0	0
SCARROW BECK	15	0	0	0	0
STIFFKEY	26	0	2	2	0
TAS	33	0	0	0	0
TIFFEY	8	0	0	0	0
THET	33	0	1	1	0
TUD	12	0	0	0	0
WAVENEY	51	0	0	0	2
WENSUM	62	10	8	13	2
WISSEY	39	7	11	12	2
YARE	22	0	0	0	1
TOTALS	473	24	31	38	12

A Comparison of Results for the 195 Sites Surveyed in 1974–75 and in 1980–81

River	No. of sites visited in both surveys	No. of sites with otters 74/75		No. of sites with otters 80/81	
		S	W	S	W
ANT	6	0	0	0	0
BABINGLEY	4	1	1	0	1
BAS	4	0	0	1	0
BLACKWATER	4	0	0	0	0
BURE	18	8	8	0	0
BURN	5	0	0	0	0
CHET	2	0	0	0	0
CUT-OFF CHANNEL	3	0	0	0	0
GAYWOOD	—	—	—	—	—
GLAVEN	9	0	0	2	4
GREAT OUSE	5	0	0	0	0
HEACHAM	1	0	0	0	0
INGOL	—	—	—	—	—
LITTLE OUSE	9	0	0	0	0
MERMAID	—	—	—	—	—
MUCK FLEET	2	0	0	1	1
NAR	7	0	0	0	0
SCARROW BECK	6	1	2	0	0
STIFFKEY	12	3	2	0	2
TAS	11	0	0	0	0
TIFFEY	1	0	0	0	0
THET	15	0	0	0	1
TUD	9	1	0	0	0
WAVENEY	16	0	0	0	0
WENSUM	22	6	5	6	5
WISSEY	12	1	2	4	5
YARE	12	1	2	0	0
TOTALS	195	22	22	14	19
			44		33

The work took two years to complete, and Lizzie was lucky to have the help of Carole Potterton, a member of the Trust, who worked with her in a voluntary capacity. Thanks to them Norfolk had the most comprehensive system of otter havens in the United Kingdom with a total of 252 havens involving 261 riparian owners on eleven river systems. Positive evidence of otters was found on seven of the rivers concerned, and even on those, with one or two exceptions, signs were few and far between and it was clear that the otter population was already at a very low ebb.

I think we were lucky in having a girl to carry out the initial work. All landowners are notoriously suspicious of strangers wanting to enter their land for whatever purpose, and the sight of a girl in her twenties may have helped to allay any fears they might have had. Having met Lizzie most of them found themselves sharing her enthusiasm, and offers of help came in from all sides. One landowner even took her up more than once in his private plane so that she could take aerial photographs of the various rivers. It would be four years before we would be in a position to set up the first pilot release into the wild of young otters bred at the Trust. But when that happened we were to realise the enormous value of the groundwork which Lizzie carried out.

In 1974–75 two scientists, Sheila MacDonald and Chris Mason, had attempted to gain some idea of the number of otters surviving in Norfolk by carrying out a survey throughout the county. Their method was to visit as many road bridges as possible, as these provided easy access to the river and many had ledges beneath them which are ideal sprainting places much favoured by otters who appear to be attracted by the security of the cavernous gloom beneath the bridge structure. As well as examining beneath each bridge for spraint the two scientists always walked 300 yards up and downstream on both sides of the river looking for spraint, tracks and food remains. A hundred and ninety-five bridges on twenty-seven rivers, including many very small ones, were included in this first survey. Out of the 195 sites, positive signs of otters were found at only forty-four.

Before we attempted to reintroduce any young otters to the wild it was necessary to know exactly what was happening to the otter population in Norfolk, and in 1980–81 Lizzie's successors, two of the Trust's Conservation Officers, Michael Jackson and Christine Clayton, repeated the survey carried out by MacDonald and Mason. Following exactly the same method they visited 473 road bridges in the county, including the 195 visited in the previous survey. A bridge-by-bridge comparison of these 195 sites revealed an alarming state of affairs, showing an overall reduction in positive results from 1974–75 to 1980–81 of 25%. At the end of their survey MacDonald and Mason had estimated that there were only thirty-four wild otters left in Norfolk, and if they were right this tiny population could have declined to no more than twenty-six animals. The most noticeable reductions were on the rivers Bure and Scarrow Beck, with the Yare and Tud also showing fewer positive signs of otters. Significant gains did occur on the rivers Glaven and Wissey, but the overall picture was one of continuing decline. At the time we found this a little puzzling, since the original fall in the otter population began in the late 1950s, probably as a result of the use of toxic organochlorine pesticides such as dieldrin. Although these chemicals were no longer used, the population still seemed to be declining, and therefore other factors must be involved. It seemed likely that loss of suitable habitat and increased disturbance along our waterways were just as important then as they are today.

If any long-term breeding operation is to be successful it is essential that the foundation stock should have as wide a genetic base as possible in order to avoid inbreeding. Thus it was that when the Trust was first set up we were still anxious to obtain otters from the wild, and since they had by then become extremely rare in England we turned our attention to Scotland, particularly to the west coast where the otter was, and I am thankful to say still is, thriving. One of the first people in Scotland to help us was a man whom I knew only as 'Mr Smith'. He very kindly sent us two otter cubs at different times, both of which had been found abandoned when their mothers had been trapped. The second of these was a male, and although it was our policy at that time to name our otters after Scottish islands we had run out of islands, and so called that particular otter Smith. He proved to be one of the best breeding males we have ever

Distribution of Sites With Evidence of Otters 1980–81

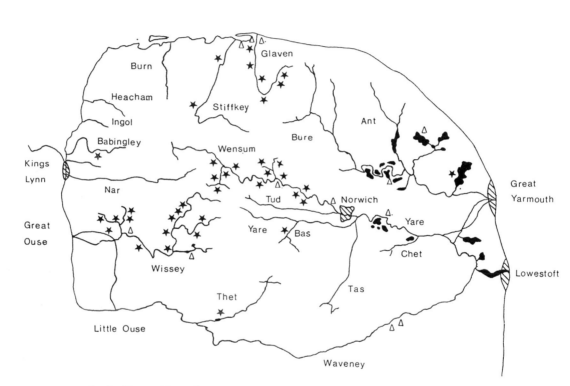

★ Positive bridge sites

△ Additional records

had. Although one of the oldest animals in the collection and now long past breeding I am glad to say he is still alive today.

Nobody had ever succeeded in breeding large numbers of European (British) otters in captivity regularly, and we knew that if we were to succeed we would have to gain as much first-hand information as possible on the behaviour and particularly the breeding habits of the British otter. The wild and remote sea-lochs of Scotland, where otters were known to be less nocturnal than in other parts of Britain, were the obvious choice.

CHAPTER 8

The Western Isles

Jeanne and I had always been fascinated by the west coast of Scotland, and our enthusiasm was further fired by my friend Geoffrey Kinns, one of Britain's most noted wildlife photographers. On a visit to the Trust he told me how he had just returned from Loch Sunart, a sea-loch on the north of the Morvern Peninsula, where he had been not only watching otters but had succeeded in photographing one from his car window as it ate a fish at the edge of the water. He marked the very spot on an Ordnance Survey map, and told me that I would find there an isolated tree bowed into a grotesque shape by the wind. If I parked beneath it before dawn I would probably be rewarded by the sight of an otter at first light.

Late one September afternoon we left the shores of Loch Linnhe and followed the road across the high ground of Glen Tarbert on our way to Loch Sunart. Below us to the left lay the Carnoch River following its steep and rock-strewn channel to the sea, while high on the right stretched the pine forests of Glen Tarbert. It was strange to recall that across this rugged ground the Vikings had actually humped their long-boats all the way from Loch Sunart to Loch Linnhe when they pressed inland more than a thousand years ago. From the highest point we could see the silver ribbon of Sunart stretching away to the west and soon we were dropping down to the weir at the head of the loch where the road follows the shore to the village of Strontian.

We made our headquarters in the local hotel, and for the next ten days I set out each morning before dawn, tiptoeing through the darkened hotel and fumbling with the unfamiliar door latch. Trying not to rev the engine I slipped down the drive and followed the coast road round the head of the loch, down the southern shore to the thorn tree. From there I could see quite a long way in both directions, and as the light increased I strained my eyes through binoculars hoping for a glimpse of an otter. The small waves of the loch died away as they encountered the thick forest of wrack growing close inshore so that only the smallest ripples came to rest amongst the grey boulders of the beach. It was surprising how in certain lights a boulder would suddenly assume the form of an otter, and if watched long enough appeared to move. Sometimes the illusion was increased by a larger swell lifting the wrack round the boulder and submerging it for a moment so that the 'otter' seemed to be moving through the water. When it was full daylight and traffic began to use the coast road I sometimes moved on past Liddesdale and down a little-used track to an old jetty, its wooden timbers grown green with moss. This was a secluded spot and gave a good view across the narrows of the loch to Eilean Mor opposite. This was also my favourite place at dusk, a time when otters were likely to be on the move and when I would keep my tryst with them, or so I hoped.

Despite days and nights of watching I caught not a glimpse of a living otter, although signs of their presence were everywhere, particularly in the small freshwater becks which trickled down into the loch. Other people seemed to be much more fortunate, and I remember returning along the north shore for breakfast one morning to be hailed by the local postman with the news that he had seen an otter on the shore eating a fish in that very place less than half an hour before. More than once the rounded head of a common seal breaking water just beyond the kelp made my heart beat faster until I realised that it was no otter.

Towards the end of that week the barman in the hotel told us about a man and his wife living on Carna Island, some 15 miles to the west, at the mouth of Loch Teacuis. The man, he said, divided his time between farming sheep on the island and fishing, but he had a thorough knowledge of the whole area and would almost certainly know about otters. If we drove along the coast to Salen he knew where we could hire a dinghy and outboard motor to make the journey down the loch, a distance of about 11 miles. This sounded a good idea, and we set off the next day. Opposite Salen the loch is less than 2 miles wide, but I remember how

An otter's holt on the west coast of Scotland. One entrance is beneath the large rock in front, while a path can be seen leading into a cleft to the left.

frail our 12-foot dinghy seemed as we headed towards the wooded shore near Glencripesdale while being swept down towards the sea on the fast-flowing ebb tide.

A south-westerly breeze made it quite bumpy, and it was nearly an hour before we reached the sheltered waters between the mainland and Carna Island which rose dome-like to the west, blocking the view down the loch to the Sound of Mull. The island itself, roughly ⅔ of a mile in length and about half that in width, rose steeply to an undulating crest of rocks and bracken with here and there clumps of birch, hazel and stunted oak. The lower slopes rising from the beach provided rough grazing, and just above the strand stood a white croft with its small barn and assortment of outbuildings, while further to the south lay two more cottages. A boat was drawn up on the beach and we ran ashore onto the soft cushion of bladderwrack alongside it. As we made our way up the slope we were met by Rab, whom I recognised at once from the barman's description. In his early twenties, tall, powerfully built and with a shock of flaming red hair and an equally red beard he was unmistakable.

As we walked up to the cottage we told Rab why we had come and asked if he would tell us anything he knew about the local otter population. He readily agreed, and over tea we met his young wife, Linda, and their son Robbie, then about four years old. Before her marriage Linda had been a secretary in Newcastle, and it says much for her strength of character and independence that she was able to settle down and live happily in a small stone croft, isolated from the world by the dark waters of the loch, on an island where they were the only inhabitants save for a few short weeks during the summer when the owners or their friends visited the other two cottages. With water piped from the burn, no electricity and only paraffin or driftwood for fuel, with the occasional bag of coal, life must have been anything but simple, especially when all their daily necessities had to be brought by boat from Glen Borrowdale, 2 miles away across the treacherous tides of the windswept loch.

Rab told us he knew of several otter holts and often saw otters when tending his sheep or going out to his prawn creels. He suggested that we

An otter's drying-out place on the banks of a loch.

should return the next day and he would take us round in his own boat to show us the most likely places.

It turned out to be one of those days which I shall never forget, for it was the first time that either Jeanne or I had seen so many signs of otters. They seemed to be everywhere. We landed first on the mainland about twenty minutes' run to the west, and amongst the birch trees, only a dozen yards above the tidemark, Rab showed us an occupied holt. The main entrance was beneath a large slab of rock encrusted with grey lichen and overgrown with grass, moss and bracken. Well-worn pathways led to at least two other entrances beneath the rocks equally well concealed by bracken and birch trees. We were to learn later that this was a fairly typical site for an otter's holt on that coast: completely safe from the most violent winter storms, dry and impregnable as the burrow undoubtedly ran back several yards into the hillside. During the day we were to see three more similar holts, all of them occupied, and one quite remarkable drying-off place. When an otter comes ashore one of the first things it does is to roll on the ground, first on its stomach propelling itself forward with its hind legs before rolling onto its back and squirming from side to side to squeeze the water from its coat. Finally it sits up to put the finishing touches to its toilet, grooming its coat with its teeth. Creatures of habit, otters have regular routes and thus often come ashore in the same places. What made this drying-off area unique was that it was situated on a bracken-covered promontory at the edge of some birch trees with a sheer drop of at least 13 feet to the water. A well-worn pathway showed where the otter was in the habit of coming ashore and running up to this vantage point from which it had a remarkable view of the loch. Through regular use all sign of vegetation had been worn away from the patch of peaty soil beneath the solitary birch tree which marked the end of the promontory.

Small pools of fresh water were abundant, both on the mainland and particularly on the island itself. They were dotted with tussocks of coarse grass, sedge and rushes and the otters clearly loved them for their tracks were everywhere and the well-used sprainting places where the animals deposited their droppings over years rather than months showed how

An otter slide in a Scottish peat bog – the vertical drop was around 1 metre.

regularly they were visited. I had often read how otters made slides down muddy banks for the purpose of play, but had always been a little suspicious of this idea, never having seen such a slide. However, later that day we were to find an excellent example in a small patch of peat bog covered with rushes and cotton grass. A well-worn pathway led from the rocks on a slope about 60 yards away, right through the centre of the bog to the top of a sheer peat bank about 5 feet high above a pool of open water, and it was here that the otters had made a well-used slide. The surface was smooth and shiny and a trickle of water kept it in perfect condition. Otters are not great jumpers, and I believe that such slides are made in the first place more or less by chance, the otter arriving at a very steep slope finding it easier to toboggan down than to climb or jump. Once established there would be every incentive to go on using it.

Nearer home Rab showed us a large patch of yellow iris growing just about high-tide mark. Once again the whole area was a maze of otter tracks, and we could see where they had made couches by trampling a bed of iris fronds so that they could sleep, dry and completely hidden. Rab told us that two years previously a bitch had had a litter of two cubs which had been born right in the middle of this clump of iris. As the cubs grew he had often watched them at dusk following their mother into the water at the start of their night's fishing.

That day our voyage took us from the muddy estuary of the Glencripesdale burn, where we found fresh tracks of otters and several sprainting places, westward down the wooded shore, past Camas Glas and on into the rock-strewn narrows between Carna and the Morvern mainland. At low water the numerous jagged black rocks stood stark and easily visible, but at half or high tide local knowledge was essential if the bottom of the boat was not to be torn out by their jagged teeth. And so on round to Loch Teacuis with its wooded slopes and sandy beaches interspersed with boulders and outcrops of rock, a deserted and secret loch hiding between the high hills, sheltered from the worst of the weather. We landed often, either running the boat onto a pebble shore or securing it by wedging the anchor into a crevice amongst the rocks.

A litter of wild otters was born in the middle of a bed of wild iris, Carna Island, Loch Sunart.

Otters are not great jumpers – they can clear the ground with their hind feet by only a few centimetres.

Then we had to pick our way carefully across the smooth slabs, slippery with bladderwrack.

Turning back towards Carna we came to the small island of Eilean nan Gabhar, or Goat Island, where once again we landed and climbed the steep shore and on up through the tussocks of sedge and bilberry to the plateau top where we found a pool of fresh water surrounded by a small area of bog. We reached it quite suddenly as we came over the brow, and we noticed at once that the water was still rippling where something had stirred it. There were signs of otters everywhere, and we had obviously disturbed one, yet we saw not a hair of it.

The tide was low as we passed through the narrows towards Doirlinn on the west side of Carna. Weaving our way through the rocks we saw numerous common seals high and dry on the exposed shelves, head up, tail up, like fat silver and grey bananas. As we approached them to try to take some photographs they departed one by one, humping themselves along to slide gracefully down the fringe of wet wrack into the sea, only to reappear, their rounded heads bobbing up quite close to the boat while they gazed at us through soft dark eyes. We disturbed quite a lot of eider ducks, and almost every stretch of shore had its pair of oystercatchers, their black and white plumage flashing in the sun as they flew off at our approach.

We learned a lot about the otters on this wild and desolate coast, and resolved to return as soon as possible. However, it had become apparent to us that with no roads much of the coastline was inaccessible without a good solid boat.

In addition to his sheep farming Rab and Linda were caretakers of the island, although Rab turned his hand to anything which would augment their income, and at that time there was still a ready sale for kelp to the local seaweed factory for the extraction of certain salts and their derivatives. Sodium alginate extracted from Rab's seaweed has probably been used as a textile printing paste thickener in many countries of the world. It had also been used in beer foam stabilisation, as a gelling agent for petfood and in the binding of flux on welding electrodes. Two main species of weed were required by the factory, both common in the

Hebrides – bladderwrack, and the much larger giant kelp or tangle which grows up to 30 feet in length, its tough stem, almost as thick as a man's wrist, anchored to the rocky seabed by fibrous roots, the long floating frond attached to the stem like a wide crinkled ribbon of shiny brown leather. On a favourable day Rab might cut up to one ton per hour, but opportunities were limited since the dense beds were exposed only at dead low water spring tides. To harvest it he stood up to his waist in the sea in all weathers and at all times of the year scything the great thick stems beneath the water. That done, he had to wait for the rising tide to float the weed so that he could tow it ashore.

Because of the tides cutting opportunities only occurred for about five days in every two weeks and sometimes less in the winter months when tide and daylight did not coincide or when cutting was interrupted by stormy weather. Once safely on the shore the kelp had to be loaded into a small boat and taken back to the quay where it would eventually be collected by the kelp factory's coaster on its weekly trip round the islands. It was gruelling work, but at £8.50 per wet ton delivered to the ship's side Rab reckoned it was worth it.

Spending his life on or near the shore at all times of the day he had a unique opportunity to watch the wildlife. At that time the otter was not protected by law, and we were still anxious to obtain cubs so that we could start our breeding programme with as many different individuals as possible. Early one winter's morning Rab and Linda, landing from their small boat, surprised a bitch otter with two cubs. The bitch and one cub ran down into the sea but the second cub ran up the beach to hide amongst some boulders. Rab chased after it and with great presence of mind took off his anorak and threw it over the cub, which was about three months old. All otters have a fearsome bite and the cub was no exception as Rab found out very quickly when it sank its teeth into his hand. Determined not to lose it, he wrapped it in his anorak and held it firmly in his lap while Linda drove the boat home. Leaving Robbie with friends on the mainland they set off at once by car to drive the 600 miles down to Norfolk. A telephone call warned us of their coming and we awaited their arrival with great excitement. The cub was a beautiful

Otter bed or couch in wild iris.

specimen and at that age was no problem to rear as it was already eating fish. We christened it Carna, and to this day his blood runs strongly through the collection and is kept going by several of his descendants.

By this time we were both in love with this part of Scotland's west coast. Everything about it was in such marked contrast to the lowlands of Norfolk where we lived, with their muddy estuaries and reedbeds backed inland by endless featureless fields of sugarbeet and barley, the majority of the hedgerows destroyed and those that remained often pathetically thin and cut practically to the ground to deny refuge to almost any form of wildlife. Even the woods that remain owe their salvation to the pheasant, reared annually in hundreds of thousands to be shot for sport. Beautiful though they are, the remote sea-lochs of Scotland have their disadvantages. For one thing it rarely stops raining, gales are frequent, communications often scanty and things like fresh vegetables often difficult to come by. I suppose it was the challenge of living under these conditions that finally decided us to invest in a rather ancient Scottish fishing boat. Built before the war at Pittenweem, Fife, she was called *Peggy III*, and when we first saw her she was laid up in Grimsby. Stoutly built of larch planks two inches thick on heavy oak frames, every piece of timber in her had been seasoned for fourteen years before it was used. Fifty feet long and twenty-eight tons registered tonnage, she was a typical Fifie, that is to say a boat which has a pointed stern and an external rudder, and like all old-fashioned fishing boats of that type she was extremely seaworthy. She had been fitted fairly recently with a Gardner 6LX marine diesel engine capable of giving her a speed of around seven knots.

The formalities of the sale concluded, we changed her name to *Glaven*, after one of the rivers in north Norfolk, and arranged for her to be delivered to a boatyard on the east coast, where for nearly a year work went ahead converting her from a fishing boat to a sturdy motor yacht complete with modern facilities like central heating, lavatories, bunks and fitted carpets. When the sea trials were over and all was finally ready and the boat fully provisioned we asked a friend to help us take *Glaven* up the west coast and through the Caledonian Canal on our maiden voyage. Bill, a professional skipper, had been born in Holland but had lived in England for many years and had an English wife. At one time an officer in the Merchant Navy, he had established himself as a skipper who could be relied upon to deliver small boats to their destination, however far, on time and in good order. Our son Stephen, who had recently been called to the Bar, was on holiday at that time and decided to come with us. We all enjoyed our first voyage, which went without a hitch, Bill leaving us at Inverness at the start of the Caledonian Canal, while we took the boat on through the Canal and northward to Loch Sunart which we entered at about half-past two one afternoon in brilliant sunshine. Soon afterwards we passed Oronsay and the island of Risga, where the navigable passage was less than 50 yards wide. As we approached the northern tip of Carna we noticed an inflatable dinghy close inshore amongst the rocks, then a man in a wetsuit and diving gear surfaced and climbed into it. Moments later Rab was alongside to welcome us. He had apparently heard our engine half an hour earlier and said he knew it must be us because he recognised the distinctive thud of the Gardner and knew that no other boat was likely to be entering Sunart. He had been diving for scallops and his first act was to give us a bucketful for our meal that evening. Soon we could see the top of the mast of his boat over the low-lying point to the south-east and shortly after 3 o'clock with Rab's help we tied up alongside. *Glaven* was on station and ready for a serious study of the otters and wildlife of this fascinating coast.

Such was my enthusiasm and lack of experience of those northern waters that I imagined idyllic nights at anchor in some deserted cove, the moon's reflection dazzling on the calm sea, a gentle shelving beach leading to the black depths of an unknown forest where red stags proclaimed the onset of autumn with chilling roars, and on a nearby reef an otter chewing the first of his night's catch. I suspect that Jeanne saw only too clearly the practical problems that would have to be overcome and the difficulties, not to mention the expense, which lay ahead. The otters were there and certainly more diurnal than anywhere south of the border. Studying them was soon to show us that there was a price to pay, and it wasn't money; there were other more practical problems, like keeping *Glaven*'s freshwater tanks filled, and this meant a trip every week or so to Tobermory for a fresh supply via an exceedingly heavy and always oily hose coiled down on the jetty, approached from 20 feet below – for it always seemed to be low tide when we were there – by a narrow iron-runged ladder. It rained constantly in Tobermory so that the task of fuelling, provisioning and watering was hampered by heavy oilskins and seaboots. We kept going up there for four years, and the otters certainly made us work hard for every sighting and every scrap of information about their daily lives. Despite the discomforts, the rigours and the frustrations, we would not have missed those four years for anything, and the knowledge we were able to gain of the otter's life and habits in the wild was to prove of incalculable value later on when we set about the serious business of breeding them in captivity for eventual release into areas of lowland England.

Glaven *on otter watch.*

CHAPTER 9

Otters and Others

Dog otter turning underwater.

We saw our first otter exactly three days after arriving in Loch Sunart. We had tied up that night alongside Rab's boat *Nimrod* on her mooring opposite the cottage and had been lulled to sleep by the gentle rocking of the boats and the swirl of the tide slipping between them. Our bunks were warm, and nobody seemed to want to get up. Perhaps we were all still tired after our maiden voyage. Suddenly I became aware of a soft thud above my head as somebody climbed over the guard rails and came aboard. The next moment the wheelhouse door opened very quietly and Rab called down in little more than a whisper, 'Philip – quick, come up here.' Pulling on a dressing gown I climbed up into the wheelhouse, where Rab told me he had just seen an otter fishing close by. In order not to disturb it he had taken his inflatable dinghy up the coast in the opposite direction before sweeping round in a wide arc, keeping the two boats between him and the otter. Soon all five of us were out on deck watching the otter, which was fishing in the small bay between us and Rab's cottage. It was so busy that it paid no attention to us, and dived less than a hundred yards away to surface with a small eel about 6 to 9 inches long, which Rab assured us was a baby conger.

An otter usually eats a large prize in comfort on the shore, but small fish are chomped up while the otter swims on the surface, and this one was making short work of the little silvery eels. I timed twelve dives which ranged between 21 and 41 seconds' duration, the average being 35 seconds. By no means all the dives were productive, and we noticed that after the longest submersions the otter usually returned to the surface having caught nothing. We were all thrilled by this grandstand view, which lasted 21 minutes until the otter finally disappeared amongst the boulders and rocks off the point further to the north.

While *Glaven* was berthed in Loch Sunart our aim was to study the otters in the immediate vicinity in order to find out as much as possible about their habits and movements, and above all the density of the population. We soon discovered that to do this effectively we had to concentrate on a comparatively small area. Apart from the mooring off Carna Island, which was ideal as a base not only for studying the immediate coastline but for trips by dinghy and in later years by a fast inflatable into nearby Loch Teecuis, we also found two other anchorages which we used regularly, dividing our time between the three. To the west of Carna lies the island of Oronsay, wild, rugged, uninhabited and smaller than Carna. At its western end it almost joins the main Morvern Peninsula, and at low tide it is possible to walk across the mudflats from Doirlinn to the island. Much of its heavily indented coastline is guarded by cliffs of jagged grey rock, while the island itself is comparatively flat and covered with heather and bracken with occasional clumps of sallow and birch trees. To the south lies Loch Na Droma Buidhe, almost

A European otter hears something suspicious.

landlocked with access to the sea only through a narrow passage barely 150 yards across at its western end. Care is necessary when entering, for in the middle of the channel is a rock barely covered at low water spring tides, but once inside you are in one of the safest anchorages on the west coast. The bottom is good holding mud and a vessel lying there is hidden from the outside world and safe from the wildest storm. The bottom shelves sharply from the southern shore so that it was possible for us to lie less than 100 yards from the tide's edge opposite a small beach of white sand and crushed seashells. Clusters of gaunt black rocks at the foot of jagged cliffs flanked the beach on either side, while at low tide the shore glistened with thick carpets of bronze knotted wrack, bladderwrack and toothwrack. On exceptionally low tides the strap-like shiny blades of tangle were exposed, while floating in the shallow water and last to appear were the long broad crinkled blades of ochre-coloured sugar kelp enjoying the apt scientific name of *Laminaria saccharina*.

Across the loch to the north lay the low profile of Oronsay Isle, while to the south forests of oak and birch swept down the steep hillside almost to the edge of the tide. Above the forest the moorland rose in a series of ridges to an escarpment of loose shale lying at the foot of a sheer rampart of granite-grey rock, and beyond was the peak of Crois Bheinn at a height of 1100 feet, its stone cairn clearly visible against the watery sky. Soon after we anchored there for the first time we explored the southern shore and found an occupied otter's holt amongst the rocks a short distance from the boat. Well-used tracks led both down to the sea and along the shore in each direction, while a series of small freshwater pools fed by a spring rising in the woods behind provided plenty of evidence of fresh spraint. It seemed an ideal place from which to watch otters from the comfort of the wheelhouse, and in the weeks that followed I spent many dawn and dusk vigils, binoculars glued to my eyes, watching and waiting without seeing a sign of an otter. Daylight never failed to yield evidence of nocturnal activity, with fresh tracks and spraint in abundance. Only once did we see an otter from that anchorage, and that was in the middle of the day when we happened to spot one swimming across the narrow entrance of the loch. Autumn nights provided de luxe otter watching, for the weather was often kinder then and after dinner we would sit, glasses in hand, watching by the light of a waning harvest moon and listening to the gentle sigh of spent waves dying on the beach. Sounds carried far in the stillness of such nights, the plop of a jumping fish, the harsh kraak of a heron; then the stags would begin to roar from distant corries to be answered by another so close that we could hear the intake of his breath preceding the lionlike roar, which reverberated through the forest and across the water to send a tingle of fear down our spines.

Another favourite anchorage of ours was a narrow inlet on the north shore of Oronsay immediately to the west of Rubha an Aisig. The entrance was extremely narrow and rather tricky on account of submerged rocks, but once inside there was good holding mud in over 10 feet of water and the boat was sheltered from all winds except from the north. With little over 100 yards from shore to shore there was hardly any room to swing, so the anchor had to be dropped exactly in the middle of the inlet, and even then the stern was often less than a dozen yards from the rocks when the vessel shifted on the tide. At low tide the head of the inlet dried out in a bed of mud, an area much loved by teal, curlew and ringed plover. We were intrigued by this anchorage when Rab first told us about it, and once we had been there it grew on us. There was a certain mysterious ambience emanating from the surrounding rocks, a feeling heightened by the scattering of derelict crofts just visible beyond the head of the inlet. It was a hidden, secret place, an ideal smugglers' cove, a tiny cosmos of rocks, heather and tide. At the eastern entrance there was a small islet, and one day Jeanne and I took the inflatable to explore the shore for signs of otters. We landed and clambered round via the rocky gulley which separated the islet from the main island. Jeanne soon discovered a well-used otter run leading down to the water on the far shore, and a little further on she found fresh spraint on a grassy promontory. Things looked quite promising as we walked on to the north-east corner where there was a flattish area with rushes and two or three little brackish pools not much more than puddles. There we found two more sprainting sites with fresh spraint beside them and numerous otter runs leading up into the heather on the steep slope of the islet. Further round on the north shore we found many more runs tunnelling through the vegetation, and as we struggled on up the slope towards the centre of the islet we came upon more well-used runs, and then I found a little heap of bracken litter and on it a lot of fresh otter spraint. More spraint had been deposited all over the area and a few feet away was the entrance to a holt consisting of a large hole going almost vertically deep into the ground, the whole site well hidden beneath a canopy of bracken and heather. I remember our excitement, for we had never seen so many otter signs in the vicinity of a holt which was obviously occupied by more than one otter, perhaps a bitch with cubs and only 150 yards from our boat! Later that day we landed on the main island and soon found a much-used run from the water's edge up over the island and into the next inlet along the coast, a distance of roughly 250 yards. Some way along the run was a dry, well-hidden lying-up place and many sprainting sites with fresh spraint. Another track led away to the north across a small promontory and back into the sea almost opposite the brackish pools. Right opposite the boat we found another run on the west shore leading from the sea's edge up a rivulet to a tiny pool of fresh water on the high ground. Soon after we found another little pile of heather and bracken litter, with spraint deposited on top of it, lying in the middle of another run leading away parallel with the shore above the rocks. We could hardly believe our luck, for this was a dream come true, an occupied otter's holt, possibly home for a bitch and her cubs, so close to the boat in one of the wildest and most idyllic anchorages imaginable.

In the weeks that followed we kept dawn and dusk watch night after night without success. We returned to the anchorage again and again, each time with high hopes and each time with no sign of an otter. Then one day our luck changed. Jeanne had risen early to make the morning tea. Lying in my bunk I heard her moving about in the galley, then suddenly there was silence and a moment later she was at the top of the companionway whispering 'Quick – otters.' Not waiting to put on a dressing gown, I rushed up the steps into the wheelhouse and there it was, less than 100 yards away, sitting on a low weed-covered boulder that was almost awash, taking not the slightest notice of us.

'Thought you said otters.'

'I did, there were two just now.'

I realised at once that the otter was on the small side, and it dawned on me that I was looking at a well-grown cub. A few moments later the bitch otter surfaced close by with a ribbon-like bright orange butterfish about 7 or 8 inches long in her mouth. She dropped it in front of the cub and almost immediately slid back into the sea and disappeared. The cub pounced on the fish and, holding it between its forepaws started to chew the head end. Suddenly there was movement nearby and a second cub arrived on the scene and started eating the other end of the fish. The first cub was the larger of the two and kept turning round, dragging the fish

An otter glimpsed on a rock.

with it in an attempt to deprive its sibling, probably a female, of her share. This went on for some time until they had eaten it, when both cubs started squeaking at intervals. Some minutes later the mother re-appeared swimming on the surface with another fish, this time rather smaller, probably a blenny, in her mouth. As soon as it saw her the larger cub dived into the water and swam out to meet her. She landed on the boulder and once again both cubs fell on the quarry together, each attempting to keep the other off. This was otter-watching beyond our wildest dreams, and although we were careful not to make any noise we found we could move about, drink our tea and watch them through binoculars without any sign of nervousness on their part. Having finished the blenny the two cubs started to play, wrestling with each other until one of them fell into the water. The other immediately pounced on it and they continued their wrestling in the shallows amongst the bladder-wrack. Eventually the bitch returned again, this time without a fish, and both cubs swam to join her. Heading towards the loch she came right past the boat, the two cubs swimming close behind her, one on each side of her rudder. We noticed that while she was almost totally submerged apart from her head and the tip of her tail the two cubs were much more buoyant, the whole of their backs being clear of the water. We had been watching them for nearly forty minutes when they reached the opening and disappeared round the point of the islet.

In the following weeks we saw them on five more occasions, always in the early morning, and once we caught a glimpse of another adult otter with them which we assumed was the dog, but they all disappeared almost immediately and were too far away for us to be certain.

We came to know Oronsay in all its moods. On the brief days of summer glory a passing ridge of high pressure would bring brilliant blue skies and a stillness in which sound carried so far we could hear cars passing along the coast road at Glen Borrowdale over a mile away. In such weather we would walk the muddy flats of the island's three main inlets looking for otter tracks and disturbing flights of mallard and teal. Curlew rose with querulous calls at our approach while common seals watched us from their haul-out places on the rocky shores. More often the wind blew from the west across a grey sky driving banks of tattered cloud and horizontal sheets of rain. Then we sheltered in one of the derelict crofts listening to the storm gusting in the naked gables and watching the curtains of driving rain sweeping in from the sea.

It was not difficult to imagine the ghostly shapes of the men and women who had toiled to build these houses stone upon stone, dragging the heavy timbers for the roof beams from the mainland and rowing them across by boat. Forcibly evicted from their land in the Auliston area of the Drimnin estate further to the south they had been dumped on Oronsay in about 1843 and left to make what they could of it. At first they built themselves typical low stone houses with earthen floors and roofed with turf, but they must have been a hardworking group, for eventually they elected six leaders or councillors and set about the task of clearing the heather and unreclaimed moss to form small fields in which they grew oats and rye. After years of unremitting toil they had finally made a reasonably productive farm out of this unpromising place, and had achieved the remarkable feat of making it support a population of over fifty people, dependent upon approximately the same number of cows and whatever extra income they could glean from fishing. As their prosperity increased they had abandoned their original crofts and built themselves better houses with gable roofs, only to be forcibly evicted again in about 1868, so that a neighbouring sheep farmer could take over their land.

Such happenings were not unusual at that time, and the Highland clearances are well known and have been well documented. But in the main it was not the Highland landowners who were to blame. They had introduced sheep farming as long ago as 1750, and had pursued it alongside the ancient cattle economy. This had evidently led to inefficiency which, combined with a national depression in agriculture in the early 1800s, caused many of them to sell to new owners from the south. It was they who pursued sheep farming to the exclusion of traditional agriculture and began the ill-famed evictions which lasted from around 1824 to 1868. The people evicted from Oronsay were among the last, for by 1880 sheep farming had in its turn collapsed, killed by a world recession in the prices of sheep and wool, accompanied by the deterioration of the inherently poor grazing of the Highlands. For a mere quarter of a century this small island had supported a prosperous and thriving little community where children had been brought up and where men and women thought they had a permanent home. How mistaken they were!

We made frequent visits to Tobermory on the Isle of Mull to shop for food, to fill up with diesel and fresh water or to pick up cylinders of calor gas for our cooker. The large natural harbour is almost landlocked, being protected by Calve Island to seaward leaving a fairly narrow entrance to the north-west. The waterfront of Tobermory with its façade of colour-washed houses and shops straggles round the western shore and at the seaward end lies the large McBrayne jetty where the regular ferry from Oban ties up. This jetty is also used by the local fishing fleet, and there were often as many as a dozen trawlers at the pierhead. As it is a private jetty all boats are supposed to move out of the way well before the ferry's scheduled arrival, and to ensure this the harbourmaster used to emerge from his office some time before to shout at the skippers to clear their berths. He was a fussy little man, and if he did not obtain an immediate response he would stomp up and down the wooden jetty shouting louder and louder and getting red in the face. We usually managed to placate him by slipping our moorings and moving out of the way as soon as he appeared, but not so the trawlers whose crews were often enjoying the delights of the local pub several hundred yards along the waterfront. I remember one occasion when the harbourmaster was more exasperated than usual because the ferry was already in sight and nobody appeared to be moving. We were doing our best to get away, hampered only by four trawlers tied abreast of each other and lying immediately ahead of us. Prolonged blasts on one of their sirens had failed to recall any of the crews from the Mishnish, but as the ferry approached the skipper of the outer boat sent one of the remaining crew to let go the lines of the innermost boat. When that was done he manoeuvred all four trawlers away from the quay, taking them in line abreast out into the harbour where he calmly waited until the ferry had left, when he brought them all back alongside again. It was a remarkable piece of boat handling executed without apparent effort.

We sometimes anchored off Tobermory for the night and treated ourselves to dinner ashore in the local hotel. To facilitate a safe return we used to leave a deck light burning on *Glaven* so that we could find her in the dark. Nevertheless the homeward journey was often fraught with difficulty. Sometimes the tide had left the inflatable high and dry and we had to climb down one of the iron-runged ladders to drag it back into the water. Friends usually accompanied us on these trips, which made things easier but no less tricky. A fleet of brightly-painted boats was always moored opposite that part of the town, many of them lying 100 yards or more from the quay, their ropes festooning the waterfront like a giant spider's web.

Otters in winter, but not those we hoped to spot in Scotland – these are North American otters.

Sometimes we borrowed Rab's mooring opposite the house on Carna Island. One evening Rab and Linda were to join us for dinner in the Clan Morris Hotel on the mainland and it was arranged that they should pick us up in their inflatable at 7 o'clock. Something delayed them so we were late setting off, but at half-past seven they were alongside, with their new baby in a carry-cot lying in the centre of the boat. Jeanne and I clambered aboard and within moments the inflatable was planing at 20 knots across the calm water. Arriving at the sheltered cove where a narrow pathway led up to the hotel we wedged the anchor in a crevice in the rocks. It was nearly 11 o'clock when we returned, and as we left the hotel we realised that the wind had risen and was now blowing strongly from the north-east. As usual the dropping tide had left the inflatable high and dry, and to add to our troubles the night was pitch dark. By a concerted effort we got the boat back into the water, and using an oar Rab poled us clear of the land to where it was deep enough to lower the outboard. It was already quite choppy when he tried to start the normally reliable outboard. On this occasion it refused to go however hard he tugged at the starting cord. By then the wind had caught us and we were swept round the corner of the rocky promontory out into the open loch and down towards the sea, pushed along by wind and tide. I was thinking that we might all be drowned when the outboard roared into life, and swinging round we were soon heading back up the loch thumping and bouncing into the head sea which covered us with sheets of spray. Linda sat on the floor of the boat with young Robbie in his carry-cot wedged between her legs and covered by an oilskin. Jeanne and I sat together on the starboard side of the inflatable and I remember gripping the material of her life-jacket with my right hand to prevent her being thrown over the side. It was extremely cold, but Rab seemed to be able to sense his way home in the darkness, and after what seemed a very long time we suddenly turned sharply to starboard and there were *Glaven*'s lights dead ahead of us. As we pulled in to our boarding ladder I tried to let go of Jeanne's life-jacket only to find that my fingers had become locked and I had to prise them free.

Normally our anchorage was quiet, but there was one night late in

September when the wind had been increasing all day. That morning we had tried to cross to Glen Borrowdale but the sea in the centre of the loch was so bad that we had had to turn back. Blowing steadily from the south-west the wind was cutting straight up the sound between Carna Island and the mainland and by midnight had reached storm force. There was no question of sleep as the gale shrieked and tore at our rigging and the heavy chain mooring cable was stretched out beyond the bows almost parallel to the surface of the water, taut as a bowstring. I decided to keep anchor watch in the wheelhouse, fearful lest we should drag the mooring, which consisted of a massive concrete block which Rab had told me weighed the best part of a ton. At one time I tried to go forward to check the shackle securing us to the cable but such was the strength of the wind that I was unable to open the wheelhouse door. Torrential rain rattled on the windows like machine-gun bullets and despite the blackness of the night the surface of the loch hissed white with driven spindrift. Sometimes the boat rolled, pitched, juddered and snatched at the cable with such ferocity that I felt something must give. The night was too dark for me to see any landmarks in order to check whether we were dragging the mooring, but just before the storm reached its peak I noticed a glimmer of light on the island to starboard. I had no idea what it was and sometimes, when it vanished in a curtain of driving rain, wondered whether I had simply imagined it. Then to my relief it would reappear, always in the same place, showing that we were not dragging. The following day Linda told us that in the middle of the night she had got up and put a lighted candle in the front window of the cottage so that we would have a mark to go by.

Fresh seafood was one of the great luxuries of the west coast, and in between bouts of otter-watching we often went fishing or laid the three prawn creels which Rab had loaned to us. Similar to small-meshed lobster pots, these creels were used locally for catching the large Dublin Bay prawns or scampi, which look like small slender orange-pink lobsters and grow to an overall length of between 6 and 7 inches. With the scientific name of *Nephrops norvegicus*, the Norway lobster, they abounded on this coast and formed an important commercial fishery.

Concentrations were usually found on sand in the vicinity of rocks at a depth of 25 fathoms or more. Rab told us the best marks and how to set the creels which we baited with pieces of fish. We soon discovered that it wasn't as easy as it sounded, although sometimes we had some luck and caught a dozen or more between our three creels. Freshly cooked in butter with a little garlic they were absolutely delicious. These were not our only delicacies, for Rab sometimes dropped a bag of freshly garnered scallops aboard and Jeanne would make *Coquilles St Jacques*.

To the north of Mull about a mile off Quinish Point lay some of the most productive fishing grounds in the area, and there we often caught mackerel, codling and gurnard. Our usual method was to cut the engine and allow the tide to carry us slowly over the best of the ground while we fished with two or three rods using coloured feathers as bait. The method was to let the lead weight touch the bottom then reel in a fathom or so, and by raising and lowering the rod tip cause the bait to rise and fall. Why coloured feathers moving up and down through the water should attract fish I have no idea, but they certainly did. Codling and mackerel were the most frequently caught, the former sometimes reaching 4 or 5 pounds in weight. Freshly cooked they were a welcome addition to our diet, although I believe it is commonly known that cod caught off the west coast are never as firm-fleshed as those caught in the cold waters of the North Sea. It is said that the warm current of the Gulf Stream off the west coast causes their flesh to be rather watery.

The Island of Mull, lying at the south-western tip of the Morvern Peninsula, with the Firth of Lorne to the south and Tiree and Coll to the west, is one of the most attractive islands in the Inner Hebrides. Otters abound in the Sound of Mull itself and especially down the west coast in Loch Tuath, around the shores of Ulva, in Loch na Keal and all the way round to Loch Scridain.

Ulva and the small islands surrounding it became favourite haunts. We first arrived there on a June evening having left Carna that morning, sailing along the northern shore of Mull, turning south to pass inside the Treshnish Isles and to seaward of Gometra and Little Colonsay before heading westward into the rock-strewn waters of Loch na Keal, to drop anchor off Ard na Caillich in the Sound of Ulva. It was warm and sunny and Jeanne and I had both enjoyed the voyage, especially the last part when we kept close in to the shore of Gometra to watch the numerous grey seals, common seals and seabirds, especially cormorants, all along the rocky coastline. It was a peaceful anchorage secure from most winds except from the south and the silence was doubly welcome after the muted roar of the main engine thudding in our ears all day. After tea we lowered the inflatable into the water to take a run ashore. According to the chart there was a house marked as an inn at the slipway where the ferry crossed from Mull to the Isle of Ulva. When we arrived there we found the slipway and at its head a white cottage. Tying up we walked up to the cottage and all round it, but it appeared to be a private house. Then we noticed a man mending salmon nets which he was coiling into a tin bath a short distance away. Approaching him I said, 'Can you tell me if this is a pub, because it looks like a private house to me.'

'And so it is,' was the somewhat dour reply.

'That's strange, because on my chart it's marked as an inn, but I suppose that was a long time ago.'

'And longer than that I shouldn't wonder.'

Despite this somewhat unpromising start Robin Cowe, his wife Ada and their family became good friends and without their constant help our numerous visits to Ulva would never have been the same.

The passage between Ulva and Mull leading from Loch na Keal to Loch Tuath is narrow and rock-strewn. At its northern end lie a dozen or more small uninhabited islets varying from several hundred yards in diameter to naked rocks crowned with a few tufts of coarse grass. With no human habitation nearby and the safe channel for boats known only to the locals the area is undisturbed, the haunt of seabirds, seals and above all otters. It was Robin who taught me how to navigate the only safe passage past the island of Sgeir northward to Eileanabhuie where it was necessary to turn sharply to port to avoid the rocks off Sgeir Ruadh. At low water the narrowness of the channel was clearly visible with only a few yards to spare on either side. The west coast of Scotland is said to be one of the few places in the world where a vessel can run aground and still have 20 fathoms showing below her echo sounder, so sheer are the walls of rock plummeting the depths.

At one time a small ferry plied between Ulva and Mull, mainly for transporting sheep, but when we were there it lay rusting on the beach near Robin's house and there was only a motorboat for foot passengers, for which he and his family were responsible. Robin had acquired the salmon netting rights along the coast but he and his elder son supplemented their income by lobster fishing. The barn attached to his house never failed to intrigue me. Outside it was a broken-down telephone kiosk full of fish boxes but devoid of the telephone, which had been moved inside the barn where it was protected from the weather. The barn itself was usually crammed full with lobster pots, fishing nets, fish boxes, ropes and assorted gear with two large deep-freeze units at one end where Robin stored the salmon awaiting weekly shipment to the mainland. He and his wife Ada had an encyclopaedic knowledge of the area and its inhabitants as well as the local wildlife and I spent many hours in the warmth of their front parlour listening to their stories, Robin's lurcher curled up in the bottom of the linen cupboard next to the fire. Despite the remoteness of the place, the nearest shops being across the water and thence by car right across the Isle of Mull to Salen on the east coast, Ada always seemed able to produce the most amazing and varied food, which I was invited to share.

About half a mile north of their house lies a small sandy, sheltered bay where the car ferry had been moored when not in use. The massive chain was still there, attached to three concrete blocks on the seabed, and as it was no longer required Robin allowed us to use it. Whatever the weather it was totally safe, being sheltered on all sides, but above all it was remote and in the heart of the best otter habitat we had ever seen. Almost every islet was covered with otter runs, often tunnelled beneath the dense covering of bracken, heather, tussocks of sedge, foxgloves and celandine. One or two of the islands had boggy areas with small spring-fed freshwater pools, and these were favourite places for otters for we found fresh signs of spraint by all of them. The drier slopes contained lying-up places while feeding sites were numerous on the rocks near the water's edge. Most of them contained numerous remains of shore crabs, the claws detached and lying near the empty carapace from which all the meat had been eaten.

In June the islets were home to numerous nesting birds. Sgeir Ruadh has its colony of Arctic terns, most of them still incubating their mottled eggs in early July, and at a nearby otter feeding place we found the remains not only of shore crabs but terns as well. Red-breasted mergansers, eider ducks, herring gulls and curlew all nested on the islands. By careful plotting of sprainting sites, feeding places, runs and lying-up places or couches on a large-scale chart we were soon able to keep accurate records of our day-to-day observations, and it was here that we enjoyed some of the best otter-watching we have ever had. For me dawn was always the most magical hour. I would lie hidden in the heather on top of one of the islets watching the birds wake up as the light came slowly from the east. If the weather was fine it was the most beautiful part of the day, and being cool it was free of the murderous midges which in summer ate us alive during the evening watches. Nevertheless it was during the evenings, usually around dusk, that we saw most otter activity.

We had little success fishing around Ulva, but salmon and the occasional lobster courtesy of Robin made up for that. One June we were joined by two friends from Sweden, Finn and his charming wife Lotta. Finn was a scientist working on the distribution of otters in Sweden, so naturally we took them to Ulva. He was most impressed and told me that nowhere in Sweden had he seen such a concentration of otter signs. It was Finn who discovered the most curious sprainting site any of us had encountered. At the edge of a small freshwater pool was a steep-sided pyramid, bright emerald green, 18 inches high, and right on the top was fresh otter spraint. None of us could understand how an otter managed to deposit its spraint there since the top of the pyramid was far too small for an otter to stand on it, and there were jocular suggestions that perhaps the local otters had learnt to do handstands. One thing was clear: it had been a traditional sprainting site for perhaps fifty years or more, and the whole mound consisted of spraint deposited by generation after generation of otters, the rich matrix account for the lush growth of grass on the sides of the mound.

On one wide rock ledge bordering our anchorage to the north we found thousands of opened mussel shells covering the whole area, over which were scattered numerous bright orange pellets the size of a barn owl's pellet, all of them composed of fibrous material from the mussels. I had often watched hooded crows flying towards the ledge at low tide carrying mussels in their beaks and this must have been their regular dining table for a very long time. In the autumn some of the pellets also contained undigested bright red rowan berries. The hooded crows were not the only ones who relished the mussels, which grew in profusion on the rocks all round our anchorage. They were the biggest mussels I have ever seen and Finn and Lotta spent one Sunday morning collecting a sackful for a gargantuan feast of *moules marinière* that evening.

Our search for otters took us to the rocky fastness of the Treshnish Isles and to the more gentle coasts of Tiree and Coll, while Rhum had always been high on our list of priorities because we had heard of the project being carried out by the Nature Conservancy Council to reintroduce the white-tailed sea eagle there. The last recorded British breeding of this magnificent bird, larger than a golden eagle and with a more massive bill, is believed to have occurred on the Isle of Skye in 1916. In his memoirs the naturalist George Lodge tells of a pair of sea eagles which lived on North Roe, one of the Shetland Islands, for about thirty years. One of the pair was an albino and they bred for the last time in 1908. When its mate was finally killed the white eagle continued to brood on its nest each year until 1918, when it too was shot. We were particularly interested in this species and in the attempts to reintroduce it as a British breeding bird because we had played a small part in the successful reintroduction of eagle owls in Sweden and Germany. We also keep a pair of white-tailed sea eagles in the Park, and although they have nested and laid an egg unfortunately it was infertile.

One Saturday in September we left our mooring alongside *Nimrod* off Carna Island after breakfast, and an hour later the massive rock formation of Maclean's Nose on the Ardnamurchan shore was abeam to starboard. Soon we had left Mingary Castle behind and held our course for Ardnamurchan Point. With the Island of Eigg a mile ahead we altered course for Rhum, entering Loch Scresort after a voyage of just over four hours. We dropped anchor in 2 fathoms of water 2½ cables north-east of the jetty, and after lowering the inflatable Jeanne and I went ashore to meet Bob Sutton, the Chief Warden. The following day we woke to brilliant sunshine with a light easterly wind, although I noticed that the barometer was falling slowly. After breakfast we went ashore, landing at the jetty where Bob collected us in his Land-Rover. Driving on a rough track right across the island to Harris on the north side we enjoyed wonderful views of this beautiful island with its corries, screes and towering cliffs of sandstone and Lewisian gneiss, the oldest rock known in Europe, alongside outcrops of 70-million-year-old volcanic rock. On a flattish area of rough grassland near Harris we saw two young sea eagles which had been imported from Norway that year. Each bird was equipped with leather jesses or straps, one on each leg joined by a swivel to a leash which was in turn attached to a ring sliding up and down a long wire stretched taut between two posts. Each bird had a block to perch on at either end of the cable and a small hut for shelter at one end, and so was able to exercise itself by flying to and fro the length of the wire. In this way the young birds could develop their wing muscles while they settled down, and after a few weeks their jesses would be removed and they would be set free, being provided with food in the area for as long as they returned to take it. During this time they would learn to fend for themselves and to catch their own quarry, and after four or five weeks they usually dispersed. At that time some thirty birds had been released and by then were frequenting all the inner islands including Skye, Eigg, Muck, Canna and Mull.

On the way back Bob told us how he used to catch eels commercially on South Uist for a period of three years, and during that time no fewer than thirty otters had drowned in his fyke nets. Eventually he had devised a method of floating the end chamber of the net, allowing an otter caught inside it to swim to the surface. Provided the nets were attended at short intervals the otters survived, and he had caught the same animal several times in the same place.

On the cliffs near Harris we stopped to look at the Bullough family mausoleum, built with a commanding view over the open sea. There were three tombs in all, one for the owner who had originally built the 'castle', a hideous Edwardian monstrosity of red Aran sandstone used by the Nature Conservancy Council as a hotel cum hostelry. The two other tombs were for his son and his son's wife, all placed in a row and surrounded by Corinthian pillars supporting a gabled roof like a miniature Parthenon. Highland cattle grazed peacefully nearby, and beyond them high on the slopes a group of red stags was moving in single file against the skyline. The island's 26,000 acres were bought by the Nature Conservancy Council in the 1960s as a national nature reserve, and when we were there eight people were employed as estate workers in addition to Bob Sutton and a Scientific Officer. Otters were quite numerous, and there was an occupied holt on the north shore opposite our anchorage. Bob told us that a litter of cubs had been born that year in a dense thicket of whin and broom further along the shore to the east.

The next day dawned bright and clear with a cloudless sky and little or no wind, the barometer steady at 1035. We weighed anchor at 6.30 and soon cleared Loch Scresort. It was a perfect spring day, the sea flat as a millpool, so that from the masthead you could peer down 20 to 30 feet into the translucent green depths. Suddenly we saw the grey dorsal fin of a large creature swimming slowly close to the surface on a course roughly parallel to ours. Jeanne slowed down to cause as little disturbance as possible. The creature was by then about 50 yards away on our port beam, and we could see every detail of a basking shark at least 25 feet long. It was quite unconcerned and even swam towards us, its huge mouth open to admit the maximum flow of water through its enormous gill slits where the slender horny gill rakers form a fine-mesh filter to extract the plankton on which the creature lives. As it passed a few yards away swinging its great tail flukes from side to side I gazed into its pale, expressionless eye set just behind the pig-like snout. There was something primeval about the appearance of the creature, as though it had been swimming thus since the dawn of time. Being a plankton feeder the basking shark is utterly harmless and would not be molested by man at all were it not for its gigantic liver, which can weigh as much as 1,500lbs, about 25% of the animal's total body weight, and which may yield anything up to 300 gallons of oil. I recalled gruesome tales of Norwegian whalers who, whenever they harpooned a basking shark, are said to have cut out the luckless creature's liver before throwing it back alive into the sea to die a lingering and cruel death. During the winter months the massive gill rakers are resorbed, and are only reformed again in February, so it appears that these sharks do not feed during the cold part of the year when there is very little plankton.

Soon after breakfast three dolphins crossed our bows, moving away at speed to the north-west. By then we were approaching Ardnamurchan Point and were able to appreciate to the full the staggering beauty of the coastline with its hinterland of towering grey-green mountains sweeping down to precipitous cliffs of black rock, with here and there a tiny beach nestling in a sheltered cove. The still blue sea shimmering against the jagged rocks combined with the softness of the air and the warmth of the sun created an impression of beguiling beauty, as if we were being beckoned to our doom by unseen sirens of this enchanted coast. As we entered Loch Sunart a solitary dolphin sped along the northern shore as if escaping from some unseen danger.

In the autumn of 1984 we sailed *Glaven* south, down the Irish Sea, round Land's End and up the Channel to Great Yarmouth. Much as we had enjoyed being aboard her, we felt that the time had come to look for a larger boat in which to continue our otter and other wildlife observations further afield.

At about this time the morning paper carried a short report about an extraordinary relationship between a Cornish fisherman and a bottle-nosed dolphin off the north coast of Cornwall, a relationship which had apparently led a fisherman living in St Ives to threaten to kill the animal on the grounds that it was competing with local fishermen for fish. The claim was of course absurd, since a bottle-nosed dolphin eats only

*Bob Holborn with Percy,
the wild bottlenose dolphin.*

between 17 and 33 pounds of fish a day, much of which would not be suitable for human consumption. I wrote to the man who had befriended the dolphin, with the original intention of seeking out the fisherman in St Ives to try to persuade him not to harm the animal. The reply to my letter was courteous and friendly and suggested that if I would like to meet the dolphin I only had to telephone and suggest a day. Bob Holborn, a broad-shouldered, powerfully-built man in his early forties, lives with his wife Judy on the edge of the small north Cornish fishing village of Portreath, and I quickly arranged to visit him.

As soon as I arrived the three of us changed into our wetsuits and dragged the heavy six-man inflatable with its 25hp outboard motor down to the water's edge. Judging the right moment between the breakers, Bob pushed the boat away from the shore and jumped aboard. The outboard burst into life, and bouncing over the oncoming waves we headed out to sea towards the granite bastion of Gull Rock. As we turned to the west Bill told me how two years previously he had first met Percy the dolphin while he was hauling his lobster pots early one morning. He was immediately impressed by the animal's lack of fear, a characteristic well known in bottle-nosed dolphins. However, it had taken Bob two years of patient effort, going out in his inflatable every day when the weather allowed, to build up the extraordinary relationship I was about to witness. The powerful outboard drove the inflatable at around 30 knots and we had covered about a mile and a half when Bob suddenly shouted.

Following his gaze I was just in time to make out the dorsal fin and broad dark-grey back as the dolphin dived to one side of our wake about a quarter of a mile astern. To my surprise Bob did not reduce speed, but within seconds there was a swirl in the water and a bump on the starboard side which, had I not been warned, would have thrown me into the bottom of the boat. Percy continued with this boisterous game, now bumping into us, diving beneath the boat, circling it and smothering us with spray as he came half out of the water to punch the inflatable with the side of his head. We sped on past Samphire Island and then in towards the beach at Basset's Cove where Bob slowed down, stopped the outboard and threw out the anchor. This was a signal for another of Percy's favourite pastimes. Diving, he seized the anchor in his mouth and pulled the heavy inflatable several yards out to sea before letting go again.

Bob explained that as the dolphin seemed rather boisterous it might be best if he encountered it alone to start with. Adjusting his facemask and snorkel he sat on the side of the inflatable, dangling his flippers in the water. Percy immediately rose from the depths, his head coming up out of the water to rest his chin across Bob's flippers, and for the first time I could take in every detail of his powerful 14-foot long body, a robust and solid block of muscle with the streamlined grace of all dolphins, the line of his mouth curving upwards towards the eye at the back giving him a slightly amused expression.

Bob slipped over the side, still holding on to the inflatable with his left hand while the dolphin immediately rose further out of the water to rest his lower jaw on Bob's right shoulder, the massive head completely dwarfing him despite the bulk of his wetsuit and hood. For the next ten minutes or so Bob, closely attended by Percy, flippered around the boat. The dolphin's antics reminded me of an enormous aquatic labrador dog. His devotion to Bob was unmistakable. At times he would stand vertically, his head out of the water clasping Bob's body between his flippers. At other times he would nudge him gently like a calf at its mother, then swim away far enough to return with a spectacular leap in the air to land close by with a tremendous splash. As the game became less energetic Bob signalled to me to join him. Putting on my mask and snorkel I slid over the side and began to flipper away, looking down into the blue-green depths where I saw the dolphin below me like a miniature submarine. Turning on his side he gazed at me through one dark eye, then, swinging round in a graceful arc, came back just below the surface. Treading water, I waited to see what would happen. The dolphin, on the surface now, began a thorough investigation, prodding me gently with the tip of his beak. If his head had seemed massive in relation to Bob's when seen from the inflatable I felt mine was about the size of a cherry in relation to the great grey bulk looking down at me. Apparently satisfied, the dolphin glided gracefully away, making a couple of passes as if to give me confidence, then quite deliberately he swam up beside me and turned over onto his back. Bob had warned me that although Percy did not like his fin or flippers being touched it was quite all right to stroke him so long as one took care not to scratch his sensitive skin. As it appeared that I was expected to do something I began by stroking Percy's chest. He lay quite still so I eased myself forward until I was lying on his chest between his flippers. My outstretched arms round his body reached less than halfway down each flank. To my great delight I seemed to have done the right thing, for Percy slowly swept his tail flukes up and down, taking me for a joyride. When he had had enough he rolled over and shot away to play once again with Bob, leaving me flippering gently along savouring the sensation of playing with a completely wild animal which appeared to be enjoying it. Suddenly I was lifted half out of the sea, and found myself lying broadside across the bridge of Percy's nose. As he put on a burst of speed heading straight out to sea I was held firmly in place by the water pressure. My efforts to break free were about as ineffective as those of a fly on a wet windowpane. Was this, I thought, how the dolphin had carried Arion of Lesbos to safety? I had always imagined the poet sitting astride the animal's broad back grasping its dorsal fin, his flaxen hair streaming in the wind, more like a man on a motorbike than one stuck on the creature's snout with his legs waggling feebly. Before I had time to panic Percy slowed down and let me go. With some relief I began to flipper back towards the inflatable, but he had not finished with me. Coming up from behind he placed his beak on the top of my head and gently pushed me down. Fortunately I had had time to take a quick breath, and was soon on the surface again, only to be ducked again, rather harder this time. Once again I surfaced and took a deep breath before I found myself being gently pushed down perhaps 10 feet or more into the underwater world of green twilight before being allowed to pop up to the surface again. No doubt Percy found all this very amusing, but Bob was concerned for my safety and, swimming across as fast as he could, he persuaded the dolphin to transfer his attentions to him. Meanwhile I swam as quickly as possible back to the inflatable where Judy, who had been photographing our antics, grabbed my wrists and

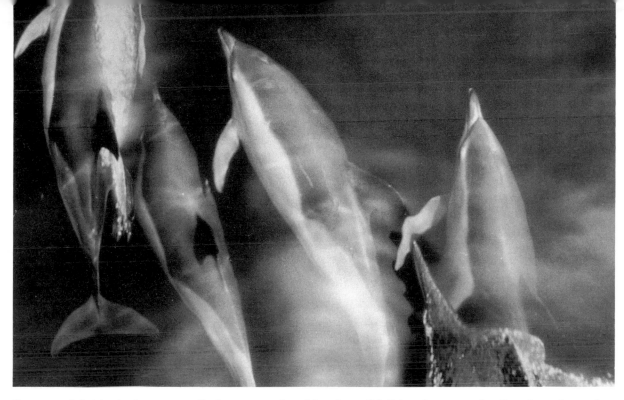

Common dolphins in the Bay of Biscay bow-riding in front of the Jeanne Hélène.

pulled me over the side where I fell in a heap on the floorboards, rather relieved to be back in my natural element.

As we sped back to Portreath Percy kept station on us most of the way before disappearing inshore towards the base of the cliffs, presumably to hunt for food.

My next encounter with dolphins occurred when the *Jeanne Hélène*, our new boat, a converted French trawler, was en route for Spain. We had crossed the Bay of Biscay and were off Cape Finisterre, about 20 miles offshore, when just after lunch we were surrounded by a large school of the smaller common dolphins. Numbering perhaps more than 150 individuals, they were split up into several groups, and to my delight some of them took it in turns to bowride in front of the boat. To do this they came up from astern, often passing within a few feet of the vessel and rolling on their sides to watch us watching them. The *Jeanne Hélène* cruises at 9 knots, and having a broad blunt bow pushes up a considerable bow wave in front of her. Six to ten dolphins would take up their position directly in front of the wave and enjoy a free ride by using the positive thrust provided by the vessel to help them along. Their tail flukes were often within a yard of the boat's stem, and I could look straight down on top of them by lying flat on my stomach on the whaleback right up in the bows.

The memory of the dolphins materialising so suddenly out of the green depths of the ocean, riding our bow waves with obvious pleasure, only to vanish as suddenly with a flick of their tail flukes, symbolised for me the freedom of a wild animal perfectly attuned to its environment. That such an intelligent animal born to roam the oceans of both hemispheres should be confined in the concrete pool of a dolphinarium, trained in circus tricks for the amusement of watching crowds, is a sorry reflection on man's treatment of his fellow creatures. I knew that some people felt much the same about our otters, but they at least enjoyed more space in relation to their natural range, and their enclosures bore a far greater resemblance to their normal environment. More important, they were breeding and rearing their cubs as naturally as they would have done in the wild – cubs which before long would find themselves as free to roam as the dolphins and which, in their turn, might raise a future generation of truly wild otters.

The Jeanne Hélène *was used as a base to observe coastal otters.*

CHAPTER 10

Back to the Wild

Exactly ten years after Jeanne and I had brought the Otter Trust into being we had built up the number of breeding otters in the collection to a point where we felt it safe to release the first animals into the wild. As far as we knew, no previous attempt had ever been made to reintroduce captive-bred animals of any species threatened with extinction in Britain, and some people predicted failure, saying, among other things, that the animals would be too tame to cope with the rigours of a wild existence, that they would be unafraid of humans and would almost certainly be shot, or that they would die from the same causes that had destroyed the original population. While disagreeing, we took their warnings seriously, and began to plan the first pilot release in a way which we felt would give the animals every possible chance. We were lucky in that from the beginning we had the support and assistance of Don Jefferies, Senior Scientist at the Nature Conservancy Council and his colleague Tony Mitchell-Jones. Don had been involved for a number of years in research into the behaviour of wild otters, the fluctuations in otter populations and, especially, the causes of death among otters, and he was also a member of the Council of the Otter Trust.

We had spent two years surveying the rivers of Norfolk in order to discover where the best habitat remained and where the landowners would view the reintroduction of otters favourably. In this we were greatly assisted by the considerable data we had amassed during our previous work on the establishment of otter havens throughout the county. With the help of the Anglian Water Authority a number of fish were taken from selected stretches of rivers for chemical analysis. These were tested in the Nature Conservancy Council's laboratories, in order to ensure that they were not carrying unacceptable levels of pollutants such as organochlorines (used in seed dressings and agricultural pesticides) or polychlorinate-biphenyls (produced by certain industrial processes). Before we released any otters we wanted to be quite certain that their particular river satisfied all the criteria necessary for their survival, including unpolluted water, an abundant supply of fish, plenty of bankside vegetation and other cover in the form of reedbeds, woods and alder thickets. We also had to be sure that the local landowners were in favour of the scheme.

Acting on Don's advice, we decided to release young otters which were between eighteen months and two years old. This would mean that their first winter after leaving their mother would be spent in captivity, an important point since it is known that wild otters are most vulnerable during the first winter after they leave their parents. As we normally separated cubs from their mother when they were around ten months old this meant that we would have to keep them a further eight to fourteen months before releasing them, and it was vital that during this period they should not become too accustomed to human beings. To prevent this we built two large pre-release enclosures in a secluded part of the Trust's grounds where the public were not admitted and where the otters would be able to lead an almost natural existence with as little disturbance as possible. The enclosures were built with the help of a grant from the Worldwide Fund for Nature Conservation, and each has its own natural water supply drawn from the nearby river, as well as plenty of cover in the form of trees, bushes and beds of sedge and reed. We knew from previous research that hunting living quarry, especially fish, is instinctive in young otters and they are very successful right from the start. The otters in the pre-release enclosures were fed daily, but apart from that were disturbed as little as possible. It was surprising how quickly they adopted an almost natural pattern of behaviour, digging their own holts in which to hide and becoming shy, secretive and nocturnal.

Don had always insisted that at least one otter in each of the first two released groups should be fitted with a harness carrying a radio transmitter so that for the first few weeks of its existence in the wild its nightly

A large pre-release enclosure at the Otter Trust.

Dog otter wearing harness and radio transmitter so that his movements can be tracked.

movements could be monitored and accurate records kept. At first I was not in favour of this idea, as I felt that a harness on a wild otter might well become snagged on an underwater obstacle such as a tree root, causing the otter's death. Don and his colleagues did not agree with me, and had designed a special harness held together by a number of metal rivets. Some metals rust much more quickly than others, so in theory it would be possible to have some control over how long the harness remained on the animal before the rivets disintegrated and it fell off. Don felt that ideally the harness should remain intact for up to three months, and while the young otters were in the pre-release enclosures extensive trials of the harness were carried out on another otter. A careful watch was kept for signs of sores caused by rubbing or for any other way in which the harness might inconvenience the otter or restrict its movements. Being made of soft pliable leather it was possible to adjust the harness so that it fitted closely to the animal's body without harming it in any way. This meant there would be far less likelihood of it becoming snagged. The trials proved successful and I was no longer worried by the idea.

While the otters were in their pre-release enclosure the scientists had come up with a suitable site for the first pilot reintroduction to the wild. It was a small privately-owned river in Suffolk where the landowners were in favour of the project, there was an abundant supply of fish, the water

Feed tunnel with den or sleeping box.

Baiting the otter's den. When it pulls the fish, the slide on the outer end of the trap tunnel drops and the otter is confined to the den and can be moved to another location.

was unpolluted and the river meandering through private estates was peaceful and undisturbed. Wandering through a lush pastoral country-side with stretches of woodland alternating with dyke-filled low-lying meadows, reedbeds and tangled thickets of alder and sedge, the river appeared ideal for our purpose in every way.

Meanwhile the Trust's headquarters at Earsham continued to thrive and an increasing number of visitors, by now exceeding 40,000 annually, were taking an interest in our efforts to ensure the survival of the otter in Britain. The otters were of course proving the main attraction, but the muntjac deer at liberty in a small copse near the Trout Lake and the flocks of waterfowl also had their admirers. With the help of a grant from the Nature Conservancy Council we built a mobile Interpretative Centre inside a large caravan donated by Roger Heap, a friend of ours. Starting with a pictorial history of the wetlands of the Waveney valley, the main theme of the exhibit is the life of the European otter and the problems affecting it. By the use of lights, photographs, sketches and models visitors are able to follow the natural history of the otter and the threats to its survival, while a continually running tape tells them about the work of the Trust, its aims and, more recently, about its various reintroductions to the wild.

Many of our visitors derive as much pleasure from the wild birds at the Trust, the variety of water plants and other wildflowers and even the rainbow trout and carp in the Trout Lake as they do from the otters. On a warm afternoon in midsummer the carp, some of them weighing more than 20 pounds, often cruise round on the surface, their dorsal fins trailing a 'V' in the unruffled water. The larger fish always seem to be in pairs and although apparently unafraid of people would, I am sure, prove extremely difficult to catch.

One summer a large eel, a female judging by its size, appeared in the clear waters of the lake. It soon learned that at 3 o'clock every afternoon the waterfowl were fed with wheat, and chopped-up day-old chicks were thrown to the eider ducks to provide the protein they would normally have obtained from the mussels and other shellfish they eat in the wild. This particular eel, more than a yard long, developed a liking for these gory morsels, and although eels usually feed only by night this one would swim round close to the surface grabbing the pieces of chick which were thrown to the waiting eider ducks. Once somebody saw it rise from the depths and grab the leg of a duck by mistake. The duck flapped vigorously and for some seconds a battle ensued before the bird broke away quite unharmed. This afternoon ritual feeding of the ducks and a large eel became one of the highlights for all our visitors and went on the whole summer.

As the nights became colder and the evenings darker the eel disappeared. Had it, I wondered, gone to the deepest part of the lake to bury itself in the mud and hibernate until the following spring? Or, since it looked a mature individual, had it climbed sinuously up the bank of the lake one dark night, snaked its way across the 30 yards or so of marshland to flop down into the river Waveney and thence, perhaps a week later, through the murky waters beneath the Haven Bridge and down to Yarmouth harbour, a journey I had made so many times in *Glaven*? And on reaching the sea which way would it turn? North up the east coast and through the Pentland Firth to head for the Gulf Stream before setting out on its long voyage south-west to the Sargasso Sea? Or would it turn south and negotiate the southern North Sea, the Straits of Dover, the Channel and the Western Approaches? In any event its destination would be the same, and during that long journey its body would undergo remarkable changes. Firstly, it would no longer feed on day-old chicks or anything else, but would start to digest its own stomach which, during the course of the journey, would slowly degenerate, providing the nutrition necessary for a swim of nearly 4,000 miles. Once in the black unfathomed depths of the Sargasso Sea the eel would finally meet its mate, spawn and die. In due course its eggs would hatch, and minute larvae known as *Leptocephali*, looking like microscopic and translucent plaice or dabs, would drift helplessly on the warm waters of the Gulf Stream towards the shores of Europe. During that long journey they too would undergo a remarkable transmogrification, gradually becoming less like a minute flat fish and more like a tiny eel, so that by the time they reached our shores they would all have turned into elvers which in due course would

Small and isolated pre-release enclosure on an island.

swim up our rivers, perhaps up the very rivers from which their parents had set out months, maybe years before. I wondered if, like salmon, they had some way of returning to the very river from which their mother set off, though this seems unlikely, since whereas young salmon are hatched and grow up in the river to which they subsequently return, the young elvers would be 'flying blind'. But could it be possible that some unsuspected instinct really does take them back, if not to the same river then to the same region that their mother knew?

The river chosen for the pilot release was not inhabited by otters, but we knew from spraint surveys carried out by our staff that wild otters were present in an adjacent area. This was an ideal situation, because it meant that if our reintroduced otters bred successfully, then eventually their progeny, moving out from their home territory, would meet and with luck integrate with the wild animals, turning what had been a fragmented population into a cohesive and self-sustaining one.

The release group was made up of two females, litter sisters, and one unrelated male of about the same age. This ratio of the sexes is similar to that found in the wild in Britain where a mature male may have at least two breeding-age females within his home range. After eight months in the large pre-release enclosure the time had come for them to be set free, and during June 1983 we built a small escape-proof release pen on an island in the river which was well covered with vegetation. The pen itself was within 10 yards of the riverbank, and in it we put two sleeping-boxes and the usual feeding dishes covered by a wooden tunnel so that the otters would feel secure by staying out of sight and wild birds would be less likely to steal their food. The three otters were transferred to the release pen on 15 June, and were fed their usual food of fish (saithe or whiting), plus raw minced beef and a special tinned food produced for zoo carnivores called ZF6. We felt that keeping the otters in a release pen for two or three weeks would increase the likelihood of their feeling at home on the river which they could smell and hear close by, and thus they would be more likely to settle down rather than scatter. It would also enable us to keep supplying food in a place known to them in case

Otters in the release pen before being set free.

their fishing ability was not adequate in the initial period following their freedom. On 29 June Don and his colleagues, including a veterinary surgeon, anaesthetised all three animals and examined them to make sure they were healthy and uninjured. At the same time any identifying marks were photographed. The male weighed 18lb 10oz (8.46kg) and the two females 13lb 3½oz (6kg) and 13lb 6oz (6.07kg). While anaesthetised the male was fitted with the leather harness equipped with the radio transmitter which would enable us to record his movements and to know for certain that he had survived. We felt it was essential to monitor this first pilot trial so as to gain as much information as possible on the animal's behaviour and survival and to see if the release technique required modification.

The evening of 5 July was warm, humid and cloudy, and by 8 o'clock a small convoy of cars had come to a halt on a farm track 150 yards to the south of the release pen, which was well hidden behind trees and a marshy area thick with nettles, thistles and rushes. Don and Tony were in the leading car and had brought with them two portable receivers and antennae for direction finding. Behind them was Rowena Jessop, our Conservation Officer, who was going to share the nightly monitoring and, behind her, Jeanne and I, followed in another car by John Wilson, the landowner, and his wife. Later we were also joined by his brother. As the light began to fade four of us left the others and silently crossed the plank bridge leading to the island and the release pen. There was no sign of the otters, which were still sleeping in their boxes. Rowena had fed them that morning and, as we expected, the food was still untouched. It was exactly 9 o'clock when Jeanne opened the gate and fastened it back. The otters were free to start their life in the wild. Rejoining the others we began a long vigil which was sent off to a good start by John Wilson, who produced champagne and glasses from the boot of his car. In the deepening glooming we all drank to the future of our otters and the success of the project at which so many people had worked so hard over the previous ten years.

A dog otter ready for release.

Don and Tony moved in opposite directions along the track so that the antennae of their receivers would give a cross-bearing on the otter and thus a more accurate reading of any movement. For a time all was still. A distant dog barked, a bat fluttered up and down the track over our heads hawking the clouds of midges, a reed-warbler burst into stilted snatches of song and a car crossed the road bridge half a mile upstream. Don had decided that the otters should be monitored all night in case their surprise at finding themselves free resulted in a long wild dash away from the release site, which could mean that we would lose contact with them.

Suddenly Don raised his hand and whispered: 'He's moving about.'

We were all tense with excitement, wondering just how the otters would react.

'He's left the pen,' whispered Don. Then, after what seemed an age, 'I think he's gone back into the pen again!'

So it went on, and when it became clear that nothing very dramatic was going to happen we all went home, leaving Don and Tony to continue their night vigil which would be taken over by Rowena on the following night.

During that first night all three otters remained on the island within 30 yards of the pen, lying up during the following day in a thick clump of nettles underneath a willow tree. Rowena continued to visit the pen every afternoon to put down fresh food, and during the first five nights after their release the otters returned to the pen to eat, lying up during the day in thick cover not far away. Apart from the nightly radio tracking, a daily search was made for sprainting sites, the first being found on the second day on the river bank only 2 yards from the water and 70 yards from the pen. The site was used again on the fourth night, showing that the otters had begun to mark their territory by the use of regular sprainting places. On the fourth day Rowena found the first tarlike spraint, quite different from that seen in the pen, which suggested that they were already able to catch fish. Mudbanks or even concrete sills beneath bridges are favourite places for sprainting sites, and on the fourteenth day fresh spraint was found beneath the road bridge upstream of the release pen. Thereafter bridges were the most frequently used sites and were regularly checked.

During daylight the animals laid up, showing no signs of movement, and for the first six days they remained very close to the release pen, hiding in a nettlebed, but on the third night they spent some time away from the area in a dyke in the centre of a nearby alder carr. This was a dark, secretive, overgrown jungle of a place where an ancient brick bridge over a dry dyke had collapsed in a tangle of nettles and willow-herb. Dark, damp, cavernous holes in the sprawling roots of fallen trees, all of them overgrown by lush vegetation, provided the otters with secret places in which to hide, and it was here that they dug their first holt eleven days after their release. Two days later they had started to dig a holt in a dyke further upstream where tall tangled hedges on each side intertwined above the water resulting in a dark and impenetrable tunnel.

Don and Tony had had previous experience in radio tracking wild otters living along the seashore in Scotland, but nobody had carried out similar research on otters living in a typical lowland habitat in England, so we were keen to know not only how our particular animals fared in the wild, but how their behaviour compared with that of coastal otters. It soon became apparent that our male began his night's activities within an hour either side of sunset, reaching a peak of movement at around 9pm and ending about an hour before midnight. This was followed by a period of inactivity of varying duration before he started moving again early in the morning, any time from 2am onwards until about two hours after sunrise, when he would settle down in his selected daytime holt or hiding place. Despite extensive monitoring he was never known to be active in the day between 6am and 5.30pm, and in the evening he was always found where he had been left the morning before.

Adult otters in the wild do not usually stay together for long periods, but we hoped that the released group would remain in contact with each other as that would increase the chance of successful breeding later on. This could be checked only by visual observation. The male otter was seen by the trackers on thirteen occasions during the tracking period, while a female alone was seen five times in the same area as the male.

However, on three nights the male and one female were seen swimming close together and on two nights all three otters were seen swimming in line astern, the last time being thirty-nine nights after their release, showing that contact was being maintained within the group.

Sometimes it was possible to obtain data on movement with accurate times and distances covered, thus enabling the otter's swimming speed to be calculated. Soon after the otter emerged in the evening it became obvious to the tracker what he intended to do that night. Strong, continuous and purposeful swimming indicated that he or she was going to have a long way to walk, for it meant that the otter was in a travelling mood. If feeding was more important he would take his time and on reaching a favoured part of the river or dyke would swim slowly backwards and forwards, sometimes stopping to eat his prey. When travelling to a distant part of his range the male was found to average around 1500 yards per hour, whereas when hunting he covered around 700 yards per hour. His travelling speed was similar to that of two radio-tracked wild female otters in Perthshire. A record was also kept of the distance the otter travelled each night. At first he rarely went far, partly because he was still in the process of exploring his territory but also because he lacked the stamina for continual swimming over long periods

A European otter being released.

during the early days of his freedom. The longest distance travelled in one night was 7.18 miles thirty-four nights after his release, and this probably took him nearly eight hours of continuous swimming.

After fifty nights of radio tracking the home range of the male otter was 9.53 miles, and this included the main river and the system of dykes and small side streams. On the night of 24 August Rowena located the male soon after sunset and after following him for several hours realised that he was no longer moving, although the signal from his transmitter was strong and clear. After waiting for an hour she cautiously began to move forward. The signal increased in intensity but there was still no sign of movement from the otter. Moving slowly and silently so as not to alarm him she continued to close in and eventually discovered the disintegrated harness lying on the side of a dyke. Two or three rivets had broken off just as we had hoped they would. So far everything had gone according to plan, and we were all excited and relieved by the recovery of the harness. Through its use the trackers had obtained a wealth of information on the otter's behaviour and movements during the first fifty days of his freedom. We knew that all three otters were thriving in the wild, and as far as we could tell were behaving just as wild otters would. The tracking had also shown us that the main river was largely used as a highway as well as for feeding, although shallow dykes were perhaps the male otter's favourite hunting ground. Most of his inactive periods, lying-up and sleeping, were spent away from the main river in woods, alder carrs and dykes, probably because he felt more secure in these isolated and undisturbed places.

Following the disintegration of the transmitter harness the home range of the three otters was monitored by checking for spraint on the main river, and this went on, on a regular basis, for just under a year. Three hundred and fifty days after their release their range had extended to 24.36 miles (39.2km), and by November 1984, sixteen months after their release, the otters had a home range on the main river of 15.79 miles (25.4km) downstream of the release site and 4.13 miles (6.65km) upstream. The final size of the male's home range was similar to that of a radio-tracked wild male otter in Scotland.

Exciting and satisfying though it was to know that our otters were not only able to survive in the wild, but had established territories and were behaving like wild otters, there still remained one final question. Would they breed successfully and thus fulfil all our aims?

Rowena continued her regular visits to the release area throughout 1984, and her records show that on 16 April the quantities of spraint under the two bridges most favoured by the otters were normal. However on 17 May there was very little spraint under one bridge and none could be found either under the other bridge or elsewhere. Such a marked reduction in spraint could mean that one or possibly both female otters had given birth, since we knew that female otters change their sprainting behaviour just before they give birth to cubs and are more likely to spraint in the water, thus reducing signs of their presence. Our hopes began to rise, although we were a little concerned when normal quantities of spraint were found again under both bridges on 18 June. We need not have worried, for on 13 August Rowena found the small tracks of a cub following those of an adult otter under one of the bridges, thus proving for the first time that at least one of our released animals had bred successfully in the wild.

The success of the pilot trial encouraged us to go ahead with further releases, and a second group of two females and one male were released on 16 July 1984, and a third group of one male and one female on 28 September 1984, using exactly the same technique. Both these reintroductions took place on neighbouring rivers on the borders of Norfolk and Suffolk.

The second release achieved more publicity than the first as it was covered by a film unit from the BBC Television programme 'QED'. Once again research prior to the release had shown that the river had good fish stocks, particularly eels and dace, and was relatively free of pollution. Bankside cover was plentiful and most sections of the river were protected under the Trust's Otter Havens scheme, although no resident otters were present. Both the Trust and the Nature Conservancy Council had negotiated with Anglian Water to implement a special management agreement for the river which would result in as little disturbance as possible. The riparian landowners and farmers were keen to support the project and several had offered to provide sites for the reintroduction.

During the latter part of June 1984 the second group of three otters were moved from the Trust to their release pen, which we had built close to a small wood and alongside a ditch leading to the main river, 20 yards away. The landowner and his wife were members of the Otter Trust and she was particularly interested in our reintroduction programme. Although we did not know it at the time, she had decided to keep a daily record of the movements of the otters during the first year of their freedom, a daunting and time-consuming task which very few people would have dreamed of undertaking, and which was eventually to provide us with a unique account of the otters' behaviour and movements.

The day before the release the BBC TV team had set up two remote-controlled film cameras, one fixed so that it covered the open gate of the pen and one focused on the ditch which we thought the otters would make for when they first left their enclosure. The camera crew had parked their control van behind some trees, 250 yards away from the release pen, and it was possible to watch the whole operation on a closed-circuit television monitor. Early that evening a group of us including Don, Tony and Rowena, as well as the landowners and the BBC team, assembled in the control van, and at 7pm I left them and returned quietly to the release enclosure, opening the gate and fastening it back. An hour later the television monitor showed us the male investigating the open gateway. After a few moments he left the pen and disappeared off our screen. Presumably he was exploring nearby, for suddenly he appeared again and re-entered the enclosure, only to leave again and disappear into the ditch a few yards away.

We could tell the two females apart by the difference in their coat colour. The darker of the two was the first to emerge, twenty-five minutes after the male. She followed the same pattern of exploration as the dog otter, investigating the open gateway and the gate before venturing outside. The paler bitch emerged ten minutes later, behaving in exactly the same way. As darkness fell the comings and goings of the otters at the enclosure were no longer visible on the television monitor, but tracking of the male continued by the use of radio receivers. He proved quite active, venturing up to 300 yards away exploring the extensive network of ditches which connected several areas of damp woodland. It was in one of these, bordering the main river, that he later established his first holt. During the next two nights he remained in the vicinity of the ditch system, visiting the nearby woodlands and the local stretch of the main river. Unfortunately transmitter failure on the third night prevented further radio tracking, but regular monitoring of the otters' movements continued by checking for spraint and footprints throughout the whole area. In order to compensate for the transmitter failure Don, Tony and Rowena put extra effort into watching for the otters, locating their sprainting sites and monitoring their dependence on food provided in the release enclosure. In contrast with the first release group food was taken from the pen intermittently over a period of four and a half weeks, and footprints at the enclosure suggested that more than one otter was responsible. All three otters were seen on separate occasions and the sightings indicated that the paler female had remained in the area of the release enclosure while the darker female had moved further upstream. As before, the dog otter appeared to be travelling further afield and sightings and spraint showed that he was covering almost 2 miles of river within three weeks of being set free.

The landowner's wife made daily recordings of the otters' movements and was consequently able to alert us to the possibility that one of the females resident on the farm might have had cubs early in the spring of 1985. The otters had made several holts in the area, all of which appeared to be used intermittently, but by the end of July it was clear that one holt, only 15 yards from the release pen, was in constant use, and on 6 August 1985, the prints of a cub were found with those of its mother in a dry channel near the holt, conclusive proof that the female had bred success-fully. In order to obtain more accurate records of the otters' movements sand had been placed at various strategic points, which would show up any footprints quite clearly and which could be smoothed over every evening so that it would be clear if the otters had passed that way during the night.

That year at least one of the two females of the first release is also known to have had cubs, and we think the second female also bred but we were unable to obtain definite evidence as she had moved on to an estate where we were given only limited access.

The fourth release was made on 3 July 1985 on the well-known bird reserve owned by the Royal Society for the Protection of Birds at Minsmere in Suffolk. This release, once again of one male and two females, was made at the request of the RSPB. Otters had frequented the Reserve in the past, but had disappeared in recent times. Knowing the importance of the site and the rarity of many of the ground-nesting birds breeding there I must confess that I was more than a little concerned at the thought of releasing captive-bred otters there, fearing above all that they might develop a taste for young avocets or some other rarity. As it happened they behaved like all good otters should, and I understand they have never taken wading birds, but live on fish and particularly eels which abound there. Minsmere has an extensive network of hides dotted about the Reserve and quite a number of bird-watchers have been fortunate enough to see the otters from time to time.

1986 was a bumper year, with five of our released females known to have bred successfully and a sixth almost certain to have done so, but unhappily on the very last day of the year we received news of the first fatality amongst our released otters. The Minsmere male released on the Reserve on 5 June 1985 was killed by a car while crossing a minor road near Theberton. An Anglian Water engineer found the body on the grass verge the following morning and it was subsequently returned to us by the Area Manager. The death of this otter was a bitter disappointment, but there was only one answer – arrangements had to be made for a substitute male to be released to fill the gap. By a curious coincidence the only other fatality recorded amongst our released otters also involved one of the Minsmere animals. On the morning of 18 February 1987 a female otter followed by two cubs about three months old ran across a road, within the Reserve itself, in front of a builder's truck which was unable to avoid the last cub. Apart from these two deaths all our released otters are, as far as we know, still alive.

In 1986 one of the females from the first release was known to have had cubs and the second female further upstream almost certainly bred as well. The darker of the two females of the second release had her cubs in January or February and footprints were found in late April. The second, paler female who had bred the previous year had a further litter of cubs at about the same time and their footprints were also found in April near her holt, which was the same one she had used for breeding in 1985. Both the female otters released at Minsmere were seen on a number of occasions accompanied by their cubs.

Such was the success of this reintroduction project that the released otters had in the three years 1984–86 probably reared between ten and sixteen cubs in the wild, and those cubs with those parents must have formed the major proportion of the wild otters in East Anglia.

One more important question remained unanswered. Would young otters born in the wild to our released females breed successfully themselves? The answer came during the summer of 1987 when otter tracks accompanied by those of young cubs were found in two areas well outside the known range of our released females, almost certain proof that cubs born in the wild in 1984 or 1985 had bred successfully, so that the second generation from captive-bred animals was already established.

Another release took place on 16 September 1987, when a pair of young otters were released on a river in north Norfolk. As I write these lines both are known to be alive and active. One of the most interesting aspects of this particular release is that, although wild otters had disappeared from the river several years earlier, the released animals, as they extended their range, began to use the old traditional sprainting sites of the wild otters, often depositing their spraint on exactly the same spot or within inches of it. Was it simply that these sites were the obvious places for an otter to choose, or could it be that even after several years the faint scent of spraint lingered in the soil or concrete and was detectable by the new arrivals?

Six more cubs will soon be moved into the pre-release enclosures ready for their transfer to the wild in 1988, and the time cannot be far distant when we shall have put otters back into all the suitable areas of East Anglia and will be turning our attention to sites in other parts of the country. Over 80% of the wild otters currently living in East Anglia almost certainly owe their origin to our reintroduction programme, a fitting tribute to all those at the Trust who have worked so hard over the years for the achievement of that goal.

With the Otter Trust going from strength to strength and its membership scattered throughout Britain, we had often discussed the possibility of opening up branches in other parts of the country. In 1985 Jeanne and I were lucky enough to be able to purchase a charming little wooded valley at North Petherwin, near Launceston in Cornwall, where we set up a branch of the Trust which was opened to the public on 19 May 1986. The pools in the otter-breeding enclosures are fed by a small clear stream rising from a series of springs higher up the valley before tumbling into Bolesbridge Water, a larger stream which forms our southern boundary and which in turn flows into the river Ottery and thence to the Tamar. With 20 acres of mature woodland on the steep slope of the valley where bluebells, wood anemones, foxgloves, primroses and a host of other flowers carpet the ground, it is an idyllic setting, and to add to its fairyland quality we have introduced breeding groups of fallow, roe, muntjac and chinese water-deer, all of which roam freely in the wood and can be seen by visitors from a series of made-up pathways. From the terrace outside the Visitor Centre one can look down the slope and across the otter pens to the distant waterfowl lake with its collection of European and British ducks and geese. Peacocks and golden pheasants roam nearby, and at various points deep in the wood we have constructed aviaries for breeding British and European owls, the young of some of which, like the barn owl and the little owl, will be released to reinforce the shrinking wild populations.

We did not have to wait long for the first British otter to be born at the Tamar Otter Park and Wild Wood, and it was so unexpected that we were caught napping. We had designed the otter dens or holts with glass tops set well above the actual chamber. Each enclosure has two such dens situated side by side within a darkened porch and each is illuminated by a 60-watt electric bulb placed out of sight. The lights are normally switched on first thing in the morning so that visitors can see the otters inside their holts, and the animals soon got used to this, hardly bothering to open an eyelid when the light was switched on. On 17 June 1987 our young assistant, Tracy, was in for a bit of a shock. Turning on the lights in the first two holts she quickly checked the otters, and to her amazement she saw that the female was curled tightly round a tiny pale grey cub. Very sensibly she quickly switched off the lights and tiptoed away to break the news to Ken, our Manager. It is our usual practice to remove the dog otter some weeks before the bitch is due to give birth, but in this case no birth was expected and the female had not appeared pregnant, no doubt because she was carrying only a single cub. Disturbance would have been fatal so Ken put a wooden den inside the enclosure before gently coaxing the male out of his particular holt. This he was able to do without disturbing the female and her cub, and as soon as the dog otter was safely swimming in the pool Ken was able carefully to block both the tunnels leading into the permanent holt, leaving the dog otter with no choice but to use the wooden den. As soon as he was safely inside it he was moved to another enclosure. The next step was to lay a sheet of plywood across the glass window and to block off the entrance porch to prevent any disturbance from visitors. All went well and we decided that as soon as the cub was a month old we would remove the plywood, switch on the light and allow our visitors to see the mother and baby. This was achieved over several days. First we switched on the light for short periods, then Ken carefully removed the plywood and cut a large hole in the centre before replacing it. Fortunately the bitch otter took no notice of these proceedings and we were able to tell the world at large that anybody coming to the Tamar Otter Park could enjoy the unique experience of seeing a female British otter suckling her month-old cub. During that summer visitors stood enthralled as they watched this most secret side of an otter's life. The first British otter ever to be born in captivity in Cornwall is a male, and he too will eventually enjoy a life in the wild, though not in Cornwall because the otter is still fairly well distributed throughout the county and the population appears to be stable. Unfortunately this is not the case in east Devon, Dorset, Somerset and other parts of southern and western England, and it is in those areas that we shall be looking for suitable sites for the reintroduction programme.

The wheel has now turned full circle, and we have every reason to hope that the British otter, while never becoming common, will no longer hover on the brink of extinction in this country.

A mother with cubs bred at the Otter Trust.

The Otter Trust

Why not join the Otter Trust and help us with our work in reintroducing the British otter and in conserving otters in general? The Trust is a registered public charity devoted to the conservation of otters throughout the world but with special emphasis on our own British otter. Its headquarters are at Earsham near Bungay in Suffolk, but it also has a branch at North Petherwin near Launceston in Cornwall.

Members receive one or two newsletters per year and an illustrated annual report. Membership also allows free admission to both the Trust's collections during opening hours.

At the time of going to print the annual subscription for Ordinary Members is £15, for Fellows £25 and for Juniors £7; Overseas Members £20, £30 and £15 respectively.

A payment of £250 will secure Life Membership and the Executive Council may appoint as a Patron of the Charity any person who contributes a sum of £1,000 to the funds of the Trust.

Please note that the financial year of the Trust is from 1 January to 31 December. Cheques should be made payable to The Otter Trust and crossed 'Barclays Bank plc', Bank Plain, Norwich.

Our address is:

The Otter Trust, Earsham, nr Bungay, Suffolk NR35 2AF.

The Otter Trust

Tel: Bungay 3470

EARSHAM
near Bungay

To A143
Earsham & Bungay

Muntjac Deer

ENTRANCE

in

out

Hide

Car Park

Tea Room

Waterfowl Lake

British Otter Pen

Heron Aviary

Private Area

Otter Pens

Otter Pens

River Walk

Home Marsh

To A143
Harleston & Diss

Far Marsh

Waterfowl Lake

Rain Shelter

River Waveney

N

CHANIN, P. R. F. & JEFFERIES, D. J. (1978). *The decline of the otter Lutra lutra L. in Britain: an analysis of hunting records and discussion of causes.* Biological Journal of the Linnean Society, 10, 305–328.

CHANIN, D. (1985). *The Natural History of Otters.* Croom Helm, London.

CLAYTON, C. J. and JACKSON, M. J. (1980). *Norfolk otter survey 1980–1981.* Otters, Journal of the Otter Trust, 1980, 16–22.

COCKS, A. H. (1881). *Note on the breeding of the otter.* Proceedings of the Zoological Society of London, 1881, 249 250.

CURRY-LINDAHL, K. (1964). *The Re-introduction of Eagle Owls in Sweden.* Norfolk Wildlife Park Annual Report, 1964: 31–33.

ERLINGE, S. (1969). *Food habits, home range and territoriality of the Otter Lutra lutra L.* Zool. Inst. London.

GASKELL, P. (1968). *Morvern Transformed.* Cambridge University Press, London.

GREEN, J., GREEN, R. & JEFFERIES, D. J. (1984). *A radio-tracking survey of otters Lutra lutra on a Perthshire River System. Lutra*, 27, 95–145.

HARRIS, C. J. (1968). *Otters, A Study of the Recent Lutrinae.* Weidenfeld & Nicolson, London.

JEFFERIES, D. J. & MITCHELL-JONES, A. J. (1982). *Preliminary research for a release programme for the European otter.* Otters, Journal of the Otter Trust, 1981, 13–16.

JEFFERIES, D. J. & WAYRE, P. (1984). *Re-introduction to the wild of otters bred in captivity.* Otters, Journal of the Otter Trust, 1983, 20–22.

JEFFERIES, D. J., GREEN, J. & GREEN, R. (1984). *Commercial fish and crustacean traps: a serious cause of otter Lutra lutra (L.) mortality in Britain and Europe.* Vincent Wildlife Trust, London.

JEFFERIES, D. J. & FREESTONE, P. (1985). *Chemical analysis of some coarse fish from a Suffolk river carried out as part of the preparation for the first release of captive-bred otters.* Otters, Journal of the Otter Trust, 1984, 17–22.

JEFFERIES, D. J., WAYRE, P., JESSOP, R. M., MITCHELL-JONES, A. J. & MEDD, R. (1985). *The composition, age, size and pre-release treatment of the* groups of otters *Lutra lutra* used in the first releases of captive-bred stock in *England*. Otters, Journal of the Otter Trust, 1984, 11–16.

JEFFERIES, D. J., WAYRE, P., JESSOP, R. M. & MITCHELL-JONES, A. J. (1986). *Reinforcing the native otter Lutra lutra population in East Anglia: an analysis of the behaviour and range development of the first release group.* Mammal Review, 16, 65–79.

JEFFERIES, D. J. & HANSON, H. M. (1987). *Autopsy and chemical analysis of otter bodies.* Vincent Wildlife Trust Report, 1986, 42–44.

JESSOP, R. M. (1985). *Status and conservation of the otter in Norfolk and Suffolk.* Norfolk Bird & Mammal Report, 1984, 27, 144–149.

LENTON, E. J., CHANIN, P. R. F. & JEFFERIES, D. J. (1980). *Otter Survey of England 1977–79.* Nature Conservancy Council, London.

MACDONALD, D. (1987). *Running With the Fox.* Unwin Hyman, London.

MACDONALD, S. & MASON, C. F. (1976). *The status of the otter (Lutra lutra L.) in Norfolk.* Biol. Conserv. 9: 119–124.

MELCHETT, P. (1979). *Releasing Captive-bred Badgers.* Norfolk Wildlife Park Annual Report, 1979: 20–24.

MITCHELL-JONES, A., JEFFERIES, D. J., TWELVES, J., GREEN, J. & GREEN, R. (1984). *A practical system of tracking otters Lutra lutra using radio-telemetry and 65–Zn.* Lutra, 27: 71–84.

STEPHENS, M. N. (1957). *The Natural History of the Otter.* Universities Federation for Animal Welfare, London.

WAYRE, P. (1965). *Wind in the Reeds.* Collins, London.

WAYRE, P. (1967). *Breeding Canadian Otters (Lutra c. canadensis) at Norfolk Wildlife Park.* Int. Zoo Yb., 7: 128–130.

WAYRE, P. (1972). *Breeding the Eurasian Otter (Lutra lutra) at Norfolk Wildlife Park.* Int. Zoo Yb., 12: 116–117.

WAYRE, P. (1976). *The River People.* Collins and Harvill Press, London.

WAYRE, P. (1976). *The Disappearing Otter.* Water Space, 12–17, Water Space Amenity Commission, London.

WAYRE, P. (1979). *The Private Life of the Otter.* Batsford, London.

WAYRE, P. (1979). *Otter Havens in Norfolk and Suffolk, England.* Biological Conservation 16, 73–81.